MONEY AND INFLATION
A Monetarist Approach

MONEY AND INFLATION

A Monetarist Approach

J. Huston McCulloch

Boston College

Academic Press   *New York   San Francisco   London*
A Subsidiary of Harcourt Brace Jovanovich, Publishers

Back cover cartoon B.C. by permission of John Hart and Field Enterprises, Inc.

ACADEMIC PRESS, INC.
111 Fifth Avenue, New York, New York 10003

United Kingdom Edition published by
ACADEMIC PRESS, INC. (LONDON) LTD.
24/28 Oval Road, London NW1

Library of Congress Cataloging in Publication Data
McCulloch, J   Huston
    Money and inflation.

    Includes bibliographies and index.
    1. Money.   2.   Money supply.   3.   Inflation (Finance)
I.   Title.
HG221.M127   332.4   75-19662
ISBN 0-12-483050-1

PRINTED IN THE UNITED STATES OF AMERICA

To my mother,
without whom this book would not have been possible

CONTENTS

VELOCITY AND THE QUANTITY EQUATION

(4) EXPECTED INFLATION AND INTEREST RATES

(5) INFLATIONARY FINANCE

⑥ THE INFLATION–UNEMPLOYMENT TRADEOFF

⑦ SIDE EFFECTS OF INFLATION

PREFACE

The usual undergraduate text on money and banking contains excellent discussions of the nature of fractional reserve banking, the money supply process, the structure of the Federal Reserve System, the history of U.S. monetary institutions and policy, and international monetary problems. But when it comes to theory, there is ordinarily just an exposition of Keynes/Hicks IS–LM analysis. Certainly undergraduate economics majors who plan to continue in economics should learn about the liquidity trap and the money multiplier, so they can be conversant with other economists. However, this material is covered in detail in the intermediate macroeconomics course required as part of most economics curricula.

In a course on money and banking, on the other hand, the student may hope to learn something about the way money actually fits into the economy, rather than how it fits into the economic folklore. With this end in mind, I prepared monetary theory lectures for my students at Boston College, lectures that I hope will become available to a wider audience through this book. In my course, I use a popular money and banking text, and simply substitute the material in the present book for the section on "monetary theory." This is the book's recommended use. For best results, it should be introduced after fractional reserve banking, the money supply, and the Federal Reserve System, and before the history of monetary policy. Alternatively, the instructor may prefer to cover IS–LM analysis as well as this material, presenting the two as competing theories. I accept no responsibility for reconciling the two. This book might also be used in an intermediate macro course, or even in a principles course, if the instructor wishes to emphasize monetary policy and the problem of inflation. It is hoped that readers will keep this material in mind when they pick up the newspaper and read about current monetary, inflation, and employment policies. However, they are forewarned that the views expressed in this book are not shared by the entire economics profession.

The word "monetarist" appears in the subtitle. I take "monetarist" to mean anyone who believes that insofar as inflation can be explained or controlled, it is caused by the interaction of the demand for and supply of money. Furthermore, the monetarist may believe that monetary factors have a significant impact on real economic variables such as production and employment. In this sense, the "Austrian" school is just as monetarist as the "Chicago" school, even though the Austrians would rebel at being labelled "monetarists." Recently Thomas Mayer has enumerated a dozen different articles of faith that have come to be associated with the word "monetarism."† There are traces of only a few of these propositions in this book. As Mayer points out, not all of these positions are logically interdependent. For instance, an individual may subscribe to the quantity theory without taking any particular position on the appropriateness of small reduced-form models of the economy versus large structural models, and still retain logical consistency. In Mayer's terminology, this book is monetarist in the narrow sense, though not in the broad sense. My own view is that these peripheral issues detract attention from the central one of whether prices can or should be controlled by monetary restraint.

The mathematics is kept at as elementary a level as possible. The material is inescapably quantitative (this is the *quantity* theory, after all), but it never gets more advanced than the solution of a single linear equation for an unknown. Simple high school algebra is adequate mathematical background.

I am grateful to my students at Boston College and to Rachel McCulloch for several helpful suggestions, and especially to Larry Steinhauer, who went over the manuscript with a fine tooth comb. The views expressed and responsibility for any surviving errors remain my own.

† "The Structure of Monetarism—Part I" (in English), in *Kredit und Kapital*, Number 2 (to be published, 1975).

WHY BOTHER?

THE POSSIBLE IMPOSSIBILITY OF BARTER

One of the questions that most troubles people when they think about the role of money in the economy is "Why bother?" We sell goods and services for money only in order to be able to buy other goods and services. Why not get back to nature by bartering goods and services directly? The intervention of money seems like an unnatural nuisance that only obscures the underlying economic relations.

The fact is that a market economy based on voluntary exchange couldn't function by barter alone. Imagine an economy with three goods: a bushel of apples, a bicycle, and a coat. There are three people: Aubrey, Bernice, and Cecil. Originally, Aubrey has the bike, Bernice owns the coat, and Cecil has the apples. Aubrey would rather have the apples than the bike, but would sooner keep his bike than end up with the coat. Bernice is eager to trade her coat for the bike, but doesn't care for apples at all. Cecil prefers the coat to his apples and his apples to the bike.

In this simple economy, no barter is possible. That is, there are no *direct* exchanges that are mutually advantageous to the pair of persons involved. Aubrey and Bernice can't barter, because if they traded their goods, Aubrey would be stuck with the coat and therefore worse off. Aubrey and Cecil can't barter, because Cecil wouldn't consent. Bernice and Cecil can't barter, because then Bernice would be worse off. If the economy were confined to barter, each individual would end up with his second favorite good, even though goods are present in the economy to satisfy each person's fondest desire. With only barter, our friends would be stuck in a situation similar to that illustrated on the back cover.

With only three people and three goods, we have to think a little in order to work up an example in which barter is impossible. But in a modern industrial economy, with millions of variations of commodities and millions of individuals each specialized in the production of just a few of these commodities, barter is totally unworkable because of the large number of situations like this that arise.

REALLOCATION BY COMMAND

In our extremely simple three-person economy, it is obvious how everyone could be made better off by rearranging ownership through a dictatorial decree instead of through voluntary exchange. For instance, suppose Bernice seizes power. If she orders Cecil to give Aubrey his apples, directs Aubrey to give her his bike, and then gives Cecil her coat, everyone will be better off.[†] However, it would also be within her power to order the first two transactions, keep the coat (along with the bike) for herself, and then move in with Aubrey, leaving Cecil empty-handed! To protect

[†] In an economy with extensive division of labor, centrally directed redistribution encounters the additional problem that it is no longer obvious how to make everyone as well off as possible without making anyone worse off. This may be too complex a problem to solve centrally.

people like Cecil, it is desirable to rule out involuntary reallocations. But would it still be possible to make everyone better off?

INDIRECT EXCHANGE

It would be possible, but only through a medium of indirect exchange, in other words, through the use of money. Suppose that Aubrey goes to Cecil and suggests trading his bike for the apples. Cecil will turn him down, but might add that he *would* be willing to take a coat for his apples. Now Aubrey approaches Bernice and asks if she will give him apples for the bike. Bernice replies that she would if she had some, but all she has is a coat, which she would be willing to trade for the bike. If Aubrey remembers that Cecil was willing to take a coat for his apples, he will go ahead and trade bike for coat. Then he returns to Cecil and trades the coat for the apples. Everyone ends up with his most desired commodity, entirely through voluntary exchange. However, the first exchange was not barter, because Aubrey did not receive a good he planned to use himself. On the contrary, he accepted a good he valued less highly than the good he gave up, simply because he believed it had exchange value somewhere else. The coat in this example serves as a medium of *indirect* exchange. It serves the same monetary function as the silver coin or green piece of paper that the worker accepts for his labor, in the belief that he can trade the coin or paper for the bread he really wants.

In this economy, there is no necessary reason why the coat should be singled out as the monetary medium. If Bernice had spoken first with Aubrey and then with Cecil, apples could have been the medium of indirect exchange. If Cecil had gone to Bernice and then to Aubrey, the bike could have been used as money instead.

THE PROBLEM IN DIAGRAMS

The situations we have just described are a little easier to visualize diagrammatically. Let A, B, and C represent Aubrey, Bernice, and Cecil, and let *a*, *b*, and *c* represent the apples, bike, and coat. Then preferences and the initial distribution of the goods can be represented as in Fig. 1-1.

The object is to rearrange the goods so that the upper- and lowercase letters are matched. This can be done by decree, as in Fig. 1-2. But dictatorship is liable to lead to abuse of power, as in Fig. 1-3.

Individual	Preferences	Initial endowment
A	$a > b > c$	b
B	$b > c > a$	c
C	$c > a > b$	a

Fig. 1-1.   An economy in which barter is impossible.

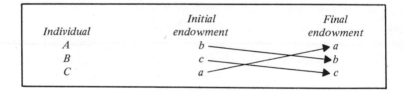

Fig. 1-2.   One possible reallocation by decree.

Individual	Initial endowment	Final endowment
A	b	a
B	c	b, c
C	a	—

Fig. 1-3.   Another possible reallocation by decree.

The necessary reallocation can be achieved entirely through voluntary exchange, but only provided one of the goods acts as a medium of indirect exchange. If the coat is used, the two transactions shown in Fig. 1-4 take place. As Figs. 1-5 and 1-6 demonstrate, the apples or bike could just as easily serve as money.

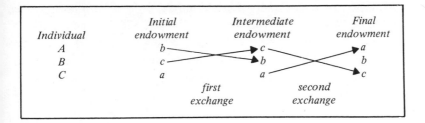

Fig. 1-4. Reallocation by indirect exchange; *c* serves as money.

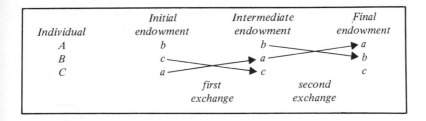

Fig. 1-5. Reallocation by indirect exchange; *a* serves as money.

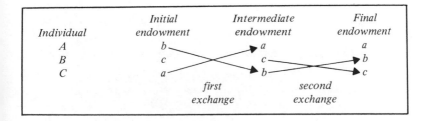

Fig. 1-6. Reallocation by indirect exchange; *b* serves as money.

THE EVOLUTION OF A COMMON MONETARY MEDIUM

Of course, you shouldn't give up one good for another you value less unless you have reason to believe that someone else will give you something you value more in exchange for it. There are two reasons this person might do so: He might want to use it himself, or he in turn might think that it has exchange value. This means that if there already is a good that is being used by a significant number of people as a medium of indirect exchange, that good is especially attractive to other people as a medium of indirect exchange. For this reason, the use of any particular commodity as money will be contagious; the right money to use is the money that everyone else uses. There is therefore a tendency for one commodity to be singled out as the *common* medium of indirect exchange, or as *the* money of the community.

Which commodity is singled out is largely an historical accident. Some can be ruled out because they lack certain desirable properties: it helps if a medium of indirect exchange is durable, portable, and divisible. Clams are unsatisfactory, because they perish quickly. Sand is no good, because enough sand to pay for a day's food would be impossible to carry, assuming it had any value at all. But there is no way to deduce from this list of properties that gold, silver, and genuine Federal Reserve Notes will have a monetary function, while platinum, tin, and authentic WIN buttons will not.

The development of money is very similar to the development of language. It is fundamentally arbitrary which grunt or series of noises corresponds to an object such as fire. But once some people have started to use a particular noise to mean fire, other people will be inclined to adopt the same noise, since there is a ready-made circle of people who accept that meaning. Therefore there is a tendency in any society for *one* noise to be singled out as *the* noise for fire. Some noises can be ruled out because they lack certain desirable properties: a word should be pronounceable, concise, and unique. Thus, "Fire!" is much handier in an emergency than "Xanhaglusho-naipoferoleaghnin!" especially if the latter expression also means "What's for dinner?" and "Good night." But there is no way to deduce from these rules that "fire" will be the noise that is settled upon and not "fuego" or "φοτιά," noises that are recognized in some circles.

The world of Aubrey, Bernice, and Cecil brings out two essential properties of the medium of indirect exchange. First, its value in exchange has to be established before it will be accepted in its monetary role. If

Aubrey had gone to Bernice first without initially speaking with Cecil, he would not have traded his bike for the coat, because he would not have known that the coat could be traded for the apples that he really wanted. Before he would accept the coat he had to have established, some time in the past, the terms on which it could be traded for what he was really after. Its value to him as money rests on its past exchange value (which he assumes carries over into the future), rather than on its future usability. This is the reason why paper money can continue to be valuable long after it has lost its legal redeemability in terms of gold or silver.

Second, the monetary commodity (the coat, for example) must be held for a period of time by someone like Aubrey who wants it solely for its monetary function. This means there are two sources of demand for the monetary commodity: first the ordinary demand on the part of people like Cecil who want the coat for its actual use value, and second the purely monetary demand. This demand for money qua money is crucial to the determination of the price level and the inflation rate, as we shall see in the following chapters.

SECONDARY FUNCTIONS OF MONEY

It is customary to list a number of different functions of money. Money is supposed to serve as a unit of account, as a standard of deferred payments, and as a store of value, in addition to its function as a medium of exchange. However, only the medium of exchange function (or medium of indirect exchange, to be precise, since direct exchange doesn't require a medium) is essential. The medium of indirect exchange will tend to serve these other functions, but they are not necessary.

Once the economy settles on a *common* medium of indirect exchange, all goods that are traded will be traded for this medium, money. Therefore goods automatically have their values computed in terms of the monetary good. It would be inconvenient to keep accounts in anything but money, since an extra conversion would be necessary. However, we will see in Chapter 7 that sometimes money is so unreliable a unit of account that it might be worthwhile making such a conversion and keeping accounts in real terms rather than in current dollars.

Provided the future purchasing power of money is relatively predict-able, it also makes sense to write loan contracts in terms of monetary units. Insisting on a more exotic form of repayment would greatly reduce the number of people who would be willing to lend you money. However, money will not necessarily be the standard of deferred payment. When inflation is unpredictable, it becomes more and more likely that people will prefer to make deferred payments in terms of real purchasing power, with the exact number of dollars to be determined at repayment time, on the basis of some price index.

Money necessarily serves as a store of value from the instant it is received to the instant it is spent. However, sometimes it is used as a store of value over unusually long periods of time. A person might prefer to have dollar bills or gold coins physically stashed away, rather than lending them out at interest, if he doesn't trust banks or corporate bonds. As long as the purchasing power of money is relatively stable, it makes a lot of sense to do this hoarding in terms of money, since it is directly exchange-able for a variety of goods. If the person filled his basement with 76-pound flasks of quicksilver instead, he would first have to convert his money into quicksilver. When he was ready to exchange his hoard for consumables, he would have to convert the quicksilver back into money. If prices are stable, the quicksilver dealers would only be willing to buy it back at a price lower than the one they sold at, since they are in business to make a profit over and above their expenses. Hoarding money instead of com-modities eliminates the take of these middlemen. But again, money's func-tion as a long-range store of value is not essential. In highly inflationary times, it would be wiser to hoard quicksilver, in spite of the loss due to turn-around costs.

The only really indispensable role of money in the economy is its role as medium of indirect exchange.

REFERENCES[†]

The theory of the role of money that we have presented is due to Carl Menger, *Principles of Economics* (Glencoe Illinois: Free Press, 1950; originally published in 1871), Chapter 8. For the history of the Hershey Bar standard, read R.A. Radford, "The Economic Organization of a P.O.W. Camp," *Economic Journal* (November, 1945), pp. 189-201.

Term to Remember

Money

Commodity money (*by permission of John Hart and Field Enterprises, Inc.*).

[†] A few references follow each chapter for the student who wishes to look more deeply into the subject matter. They are certainly not meant to be exhaustive.

THE DETERMINATION
OF THE PRICE LEVEL

THE PRICE LEVEL

When we accept money in exchange for the sweat of our brow, or for anything else we are reluctant to part with, it is because we expect to be able to use it to buy goods we value more highly. If prices all doubled, we would value a dollar only half as much as otherwise.

Since all prices don't move together, it is not always clear just how much the value of money has changed. People have differing consumption patterns, so that money may have risen in value to one person at the same time it has fallen for someone else. Furthermore, prices in different geographic areas will move differently. Nevertheless, it is often useful to have an index of prices that, while imperfect, will still approximately capture important changes in the general level of prices.

In order to compute a price index, we first have to settle on some year in which money had "standard" purchasing power. Our price index will have value 1.00 in this year (call it year 1). If prices then all double, we will want our index to go up to 2.00. If they all fall to a quarter of their year 1 value, we will want the index to register 0.25.

One index with this property could be obtained by taking the average of all prices and then computing the ratio of this average for the current year to its value for the base year. Suppose there are n goods in all, named a, b, c, d, and so on up to z. Let P_a^1 represent the price of good a in year 1, P_b^1 the price of good b in year 1, P_a^2 the price of good a in year 2, and so forth. Then this price index for year 2 would be given by

$$P = \frac{(P_a^2 + P_b^2 + \cdots + P_z^2)/n}{(P_a^1 + P_b^1 + \cdots + P_z^1)/n} \qquad \text{(wrong)} \qquad (2\text{-}1)$$

We may simplify this formula by multiplying both numerator and denominator by n:

$$P = \frac{P_a^2 + P_b^2 + \cdots + P_z^2}{P_a^1 + P_b^1 + \cdots + P_z^1} \qquad \text{(wrong)} \qquad (2\text{-}2)$$

This price index candidate has the correct property that if all prices are the same in year 2 as they were in year 1, it will be 1.00, if all prices exactly double it will be 2.00, and so forth. However, it is wrong because it gives equal weight to every good regardless of how important it is in the economy. This problem matters if all prices don't move together in exactly the same proportion.

We can solve this problem by weighting each price by the quantity of the corresponding good that is produced and consumed. Let Q_a^1 be the quantity of good a in year 1, and so on, as with prices. Our new index candidate is

$$P = \frac{Q_a^2 P_a^2 + Q_b^2 P_b^2 + \cdots + Q_z^2 P_z^2}{Q_a^1 P_a^1 + Q_b^1 P_b^1 + \cdots + Q_z^1 P_z^1} \qquad \text{(worse)} \qquad (2\text{-}3)$$

This index is still defective. Its problem is that it doesn't distinguish between changes in prices and changes in quantities. For instance, if all prices remained constant while all quantities doubled (because of the growth of the economy, for instance), it would register 2.00, just as it would if all quantities remained the same and all prices doubled. What we have actually constructed is an index of the dollar value of output, rather than of prices.

In order to get a proper price index, we must use the same quantities to weight the year 2 prices that we used to weight the year 1 prices. Such a correct formula is

$$P = \frac{Q_a^1 P_a^2 + Q_b^1 P_b^2 + Q_c^1 P_c^2 + \cdots + Q_z^1 P_z^2}{Q_a^1 P_a^1 + Q_b^1 P_b^1 + Q_c^1 P_c^1 + \cdots + Q_z^1 P_z^1} \qquad \text{(right)} \qquad (2\text{-}4)$$

Here we have used the quantities for year 1 in both the numerator and denominator. It would make just as much sense to have used the quantities for year 2. Doing so would give a slightly different numerical value for the price index, but would be equally valid.

Let us take an example with three goods *a, b,* and *c.* Between year 1 and year 2, the price of *a* rises from \$10 to \$15, the price of *b* falls from \$14 to \$11, and the price of *c* stays constant at \$2. If in year 1, 6 units of *a*, 7 units of *b*, and 21 units of *c* are sold, we could compute the price level in year 2 relative to that in year 1 as

$$P = \frac{Q_a^1 P_a^2 + Q_b^1 P_b^2 + Q_c^1 P_c^2}{Q_a^1 P_a^1 + Q_b^1 P_b^1 + Q_c^1 P_c^1}$$

$$= \frac{(6)(15) + (7)(11) + (21)(2)}{(6)(10) + (7)(14) + (21)(2)}$$

$$= \frac{90 + 77 + 42}{60 + 98 + 42}$$

$$= \frac{209}{200}$$

$$= 1.045 \qquad (2\text{-}5)$$

The inflation rate can be computed from the price index by $\Delta P/P$. The symbol delta (Δ) indicates the change in the variable it precedes, so that ΔP means "the change in P" and $\Delta P/P$ means "the percentage change in *P*." The price index started off as 1.00 in year 1 and rose to 1.045 in year 2, so $\Delta P = 0.045$. Therefore, $\Delta P/P = 0.45/1.00 = 0.045$ or 4.5%. Although the price of the first good went up while that of the second good went down and that of the third good didn't change, on average prices rose by 4.5%.

If we had felt like using the quantities for year 2, we would have gotten a somewhat different answer. Suppose that in year 2, 7 units of *a*, 8 units of *b*, and 23 units of *c* are sold. Using these quantities, the price index becomes

$$P = \frac{Q_a^2 P_a^2 + Q_b^2 P_b^2 + Q_c^2 P_c^2}{Q_a^2 P_a^1 + Q_b^2 P_b^1 + Q_c^2 P_c^1}$$

$$= \frac{(7)(15) + (8)(11) + (23)(2)}{(7)(10) + (8)(14) + (23)(2)}$$

$$= \frac{239}{228}$$

$$= 1.048 \tag{2-6}$$

or 4.8% inflation for the year, instead of 4.5%. The fact that we can obtain two different inflation rates using the same price data just shows that no price index should be taken too literally.

Whether the first-period quantities or the second-period quantities are used is the distinction between the so-called "Paasche" and "Lespeyres" types of price index. No one can ever remember which is which. In any event, one is just as good in principle as the other (or one is just as bad as the other, if you prefer). In practice, an up-to-the-minute price index is easier to compute using pre-established quantity weights, so the Lespeyres index, which uses the earlier quantities, is more commonly encountered.

In these examples it didn't matter whether or not we divided by *P* to compute the inflation rate, since it started off at unity in year 1. However, if *P* had risen to 3.00 by year 10, and then rose to 3.21 by year 11, the inflation rate would have been $(3.21 - 3.00)/3.00 = 0.21/3.00 = 0.07$, or 7%.

There are several different price indices published, and the inflation rates computed from them will differ slightly. The best indicator of the cost of living is the Consumer Price Index (CPI), which is calculated monthly by the Bureau of Labor Statistics in the Labor Department. It is based strictly on retail prices for consumption goods. The Wholesale Price Index (WPI) is based on the wholesale prices of a few standard commodities, only some of which are directly related to consumption goods. Its advantage is that it is easy to reconstruct for historical periods. It is also thought to be more sensitive to current developments. The GNP deflator is computed by the Commerce Department in the course of estimating real and current-dollar gross national product for the national income accounts. It takes into account the prices of both consumption and investment goods, so it is not as good an index of the cost of living as the CPI. However, it serves as a useful check on the CPI, since the two are computed entirely independently.

Problem 2-1

Compute the price level in year 2 using the following data:

	Good a		Good b	
	Year 1	Year 2	Year 1	Year 2
Price ($)	11	12	7	9
Quantity (units)	2	1	4	5

Problem 2-2

If P rises from 2.50 to 3.00 in one year, what is the percentage inflation rate?

[*Note*: Solutions are gathered at the end of the book. For best results, the student should work through each problem to a numerical solution *before* looking at the answers.]

NOMINAL VERSUS REAL CASH BALANCES

Now that we have a price index, there are two ways we can measure the quantity of money. There are *nominal* cash balances and *real* cash balances. This is a crucial distinction. By "nominal" cash balances we mean a quantity of money measured in ordinary, current dollars. "Real" cash balances, on the other hand, are measured in terms of purchasing power. In order to find this purchasing power, we divide the nominal quantity by the price index. Real cash balances will then be measured in terms of the purchasing power the dollar had in the base year for our price index.

We will use an uppercase M to represent money when we want it in nominal terms and a lowercase m when we want it in real terms. We can convert from one to the other simply by multiplying or dividing by the price index P:

$$M = mP \tag{2-7}$$

$$m = \frac{M}{P} \tag{2-8}$$

In Chapter 3, we will similarly use the lowercase letters t and y to represent the real volume of transactions and the real level of income, respectively. These values are likewise arrived at by dividing nominal transactions and nominal income by the current value of the price index.

If we happen to be considering the base year for our price index, the year in which we regard money as having had "standard" purchasing power, m and M will be equal, since P will equal unity. If there has been inflation since the base year so that P has become greater than unity, m will be less than M. If there has been deflation, m will be greater than M.

THE DETERMINATION OF THE PRICE LEVEL

P is the price of goods in general in terms of money, so $1/P$ may be thought of as the price of money in terms of goods. The fundamental assumption of the "monetarist" or "quantity theory" type of monetary theory is that this price of money ultimately gets determined by the interaction of the demand for and supply of money, much as the price of any other good is determined by its demand and supply.

In Chapter 1, it was noted that a positive demand to hold money arises along with the use of money as a medium of indirect exchange. This demand is essentially a demand for real cash balances. For instance, if prices all doubled and then stayed at their new level, people would want to hold exactly twice as many nominal cash balances on average as they would otherwise, since it would take twice as many dollars to conduct any given real transaction. We should therefore regard the demand for money as being relatively fixed in real terms, rather than in nominal terms. We will represent this demand for real cash balances as m^D. The demand for nominal cash balances is then given by $M^D = Pm^D$.

Today our money supply consists essentially of paper fiat money and demand deposits (checking accounts) backed by this paper money. The Federal Reserve System together with the commercial banks and the preferences of the public for currency versus demand deposits determine the supply of this money, in nominal terms, as so many current dollars. We will represent this supply of nominal cash balances as M^S.†

In order to equate supply and demand, we must use common units, either real values or current dollars. If we choose current dollars, we have

$$M^S = M^D \tag{2-9}$$

or

$$M^S = Pm^D \tag{2-10}$$

†Milton Friedman prefers to define the money supply as M_2, the sum of currency, demand deposits, *and* time deposits at commercial banks. We finesse this nuance, and stick to the above definition, known as M_1.

We divide by the demand for real cash balances in order to obtain the price level as the ratio of the supply of nominal cash balances to the demand for real cash balances:

$$P = \frac{M^S}{m^D} \tag{2-11}$$

Formula (2-11) gives the equilibrium price level that equates monetary supply and demand. It implies that if m^D is constant, the equilibrium price level will be proportional to the nominal money supply. Doubling the money supply will double the equilibrium price level. This proportionality between the nominal quantity of money and the equilibrium price level is the fundamental proposition of what is known as the "quantity theory of money," or the "quantity theory" for short. It might actually have been more appropriate to have called it the "quantity of money theory of the price level" instead.

THE ADJUSTMENT PROCESS

If M^S increases relative to m^D, what makes P rise? First let us take the case of an increase in the money supply due to increased counterfeiting. Every dollar a counterfeiter prints makes him feel a dollar wealthier. He will use this new income to increase his standard of living above what it would have been otherwise. In order to do this, he must outbid other potential buyers of goods and services, because his printing of money does not bring any additional goods onto the market.

By itself this rise probably would push the general price level only a small fraction of the way to its new equilibrium. However, the people from whom he bought the goods also feel richer now than they would have without the increase in M^S, since they have received higher prices for the goods they sell, while the goods they buy have not yet risen, at least not as much as the goods they sell. When they try to increase their standard of living, they will push up the prices of the goods they buy. This process continues for round after round of additional small price rises.

It is easy to see that this process will not increase all prices in exactly the same proportion. The goods the counterfeiter buys will generally be higher in price relative to other goods as long as his presses remain in motion. The same is true of the goods bought with the profits of the merchants who provide him with goods and services. Even after the Secret Service gets wise to him and he has to retire, the price effects of his actions will spread like ripples throughout the economy. The former relations between prices will never be exactly restored. The older quantity theorists sometimes tended to exaggerate the uniformity of the price rise that a monetary disturbance would bring about.

The same process would occur if the Treasury, instead of a counterfeiter, were to print the new money. By printing money to finance expenditures instead of taxing the public directly, the Treasury would increase its purchasing power without making the public feel any poorer, at least not until after the purchasing power of their cash balances had mysteriously fallen.

Under a gold standard, the process is similar, with the miner who discovers a new gold deposit replacing the counterfeiter or the government. However, there are a number of different cases. In the simplest case, suppose that the miner just trips over a large gold nugget without any significant expenditure of resources, and that there is no demand for gold as a commodity for use in jewelry and industry. Here the miner feels richer, while the real goods and services available in the community have not changed, so prices get bid up, starting with the goods he buys. The price rise should be roughly in proportion to the amount his discovery adds to the gold money supply.

Suppose instead that the resources he expends to find the gold are almost exactly equal in value to the gold he obtains. For each 1.000 grams of gold he extracts, he must spend 0.999 grams of gold worth of dynamite, picks, labor, and refining chemicals. In this case, he feels no richer (or only negligibly richer). Meanwhile the community is actually poorer by the value of the resources he expended, just as surely as if the owners of these resources had been ordered to dump them down a hole in the ground. Nevertheless these owners do not feel any poorer, since they receive payment in gold for the resources they give up. Consequently there arises a disparity between how rich the community feels and how rich it really is, which again serves to bid prices up. Only instead of starting with the consumption goods the miner buys, the inflation now starts with the productive resources he bids away from alternative uses—the dynamite, picks, labor, and chemicals. The higher prices of these resources drive up costs in other industries, and ultimately the prices of consumer goods. Again, the process does not end until the price level has gone up in the proportion by which the new gold has added to the money supply, assuming the demand for real cash balances remains constant.

Now let us consider the case in which there is a demand for gold as a commodity. This commodity demand for gold (as contrasted with the monetary demand) will tend to lessen the impact of gold production on the price level. If this demand behaves in the usual way, it decreases with the price of gold in terms of other goods. That is, the more expensive gold is, the less of it people can afford to use for bathroom fixtures, dental fillings, and the like. The price index P is the average price of goods in terms of money, which we are presently assuming to be gold. Therefore, $1/P$ can be thought of as the price of gold in terms of goods in general. For the sake of illustration, if prices in terms of gold money all double, then twice as many grams of gold will be given in exchange for a bushel of wheat. But by the same token, only half as many bushels of wheat will be given in exchange for a gram of gold. The commodity demand for gold, in terms of this price, of gold, will probably have the ordinary downward slope of a demand curve, as shown in Fig. 2-1. The decreasing relationship in Fig. 2-1 means that the demand for gold will *increase* with P, the price of goods in terms of gold, as in Fig. 2-2.

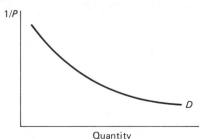

Fig. 2-1. Commodity demand for gold.

Fig. 2-2. Commodity demand for gold.

This increasing relation means that as prices rise due to the new gold strike, some gold will be diverted from monetary employment to commodity employment. Therefore, the money supply will not go up in proportion to the total increase in the gold stock, but only by some fraction of this increase. The price level will increase by an amount consistent with the increase in the monetary gold stock, but not in proportion to the increase in the total gold stock. In this way, the commodity demand lessens the impact of the change in the gold stock on the price level.

The same dampening effect would work in reverse if the gold stock were to decrease relative to m^D. This could come about either through an actual reduction in the gold supply—for instance, if a ship laden with gold were to sink—or, as is more likely, if the gold stock stayed relatively constant while m^D grew due to the secular growth of the economy. The ensuing decline in the price level (rise in the price of gold in terms of goods) would bring gold out of commodity employment and cushion the price decline.

Most of the U.S. money supply is created in the form of demand deposits as commercial banks lend to businesses or buy securities, rather than through the actions of counterfeiters, the government's printing presses, or gold miners. However, this type of money creation still causes an increase in perceived wealth without increasing the real resources available to the community, and therefore is also inflationary. Part of the first round increase in perceived wealth goes to the stockholders of the banks. The banks have increased earning assets, yet do not have to pay interest on the new demand deposits. Therefore, they have increased profits, which sooner or later get passed on to the banks' owners, the shareholders. (Most banks are prohibited by law from passing the earnings on their assets on to their checking customers, as competition would otherwise force them to do. Fortunately, loopholes have begun to appear in this law in the past few years.) The rest of the first round increase goes to the business firms, home buyers, and so forth, who are able to obtain loans at lower interest rates than they would otherwise have had to pay.

WALRAS' LAW

The income effects discussed above get prices moving in the direction of equilibrium whenever M^S changes relative to m^D, but what guarantees that they will continue until M^S just equals Pm^D? There is no simple market for money in which the price of money, $1/P$, gets determined. After all, P is just an average of the prices of various commodities. Each of these prices is determined by supply and demand in its own market. What reason is there to expect that the individual prices that get determined in individual commodity markets will, when averaged together and reciprocated, give exactly the $1/P$ that equates the supply and demand for money? What if the two ways of determining P are different?

Walras' law[†] solves this problem. It is based on the notion that people produce goods for sale in order to buy other goods. For each person, the supply he introduces onto some markets is exactly equal in value to the demand he expresses on other markets. When we sum over all markets and over all individuals, total supply must just equal total demand.

In order to be complete, we must take into account the demand and supply of money. When a worker sells his labor, he may be trying to increase his holdings of money, rather than to increase his consumption. Therefore, total supply equals total demand only provided we add in the supply and demand for money. This is the essence of Walras' law.

What then if the supply and demand for nominal cash balances are

[†]Named after the turn-of-the-century French-born economist Leon Walras (pronounced vahl-rahss, according to Dr. Shavell).

out of equality? If the supply of money exceeds the demand for money, by Walras' law, the total demand for ordinary (nonmonetary) goods must exceed the total supply of ordinary goods. This in turn means that demand must exceed supply in at least one goods market. Excess demand tends to drive the price of goods up, so it follows that at least one ordinary price has upward pressure on it as a consequence of the excess supply of money. This in turn acts to drive the price index up, and pulls the demand and supply of money into equilibrium through inflation.

Similarly, if P is too high so that there is an excess demand for money, Walras' law implies that there will be an excess of total supply over total demand in the markets for ordinary goods. Therefore, there must be downward pressure on at least one price. This drives the price index down, and brings the demand and supply of money into equilibrium through *de*flation.

If there is an excess supply of money, the corresponding excess demand for goods may appear as an excess demand for future goods, rather than for present goods. That is, consumers may be planning to consume more than producers are planning to produce at some time in the more or less distant future. If people provided for the future by simply hoarding money, the full inflationary pressure corresponding to the present excess supply of money would not appear in the goods market for several months or even several years. However, in an economy such as ours with a well-developed financial system, it is more advantageous to provide for the future by lending surplus money out at interest, either directly by buying corporate bonds, or indirectly through a thrift institution. Meanwhile, producers are borrowing money in today's market in order to provide for future production. Therefore, an excess demand for future goods will be reflected today, in the financial markets, as an excess demand for bonds. This excess demand for bonds will tend to drive their prices up or, equivalently, their market interest rates down.[†] As interest rates fall, the excess demand will be shifted to the markets for current factors of production, such as labor and materials, because the firms that borrow money at the reduced interest rates are in a position to bid these factors away from

[†]A bond's yield to maturity (the effective interest rate you get by buying it at its current price) falls as its price rises, and vice versa.

other firms. Finally, as this disequilibrium is removed through increases in wages and the prices of materials, a new disequilibrium will appear in the market for current consumption goods, due to the increased purchasing power of workers and the owners of raw materials on the one hand and increased costs of production on the other. Through this somewhat round-about route, the excess supply of money ends up as an excess demand for current goods and services, and prices must rise until the demand and supply for money are once again in equilibrium. In a financially equipped economy, therefore, we do not need to wait for years for Walras' law to force an excess demand for current goods to appear.

THE DEMAND FOR MONEY

The demand for real cash balances has two principal determinants. First, there is the real quantity of transactions that must be conducted with the use of money. The actual changing of hands doesn't tie up any money, since this takes only an instant. Where the demand for money arises is in the balances that lie "idle" between when they are received and when they are expended. In the example of Chapter 1, Aubrey's owner-ship of the coat, from the time he receives it from Bernice until he gives it to Cecil, illustrates this demand for money.

Second, there is the cost of holding money. If you were to reduce your holdings of non-interest-bearing dollar bills or demand deposits by one dollar on average over the year, you would be able to earn interest on that dollar by depositing it in a savings account or using it to help buy an interest-earning security. The interest you forego by holding money is not an out-of-pocket expense, but rather what economists call an opportunity cost. The higher this opportunity cost of money, the more effort you will put into planning your cash flows in order to earn interest, and conse-quently, the lower your average holdings of real cash balances.

It is not settled which index of real transactions most closely deter-mines m^D. Even if we had records of all transactions (which we don't), their sum might not be appropriate, since people probably take foregone interest into account more for large transactions than for small transac-tions. It makes sense to wait until just before your rent bill is due to withdraw money from your savings account to meet it, whereas it does not make sense if all you're buying is the evening newspaper. A large number of small transactions probably result in larger m^D than a few large transactions with the same total value.

Total income is usually assumed to be a fair index of this transactions demand for money, although a case could also be made for consumption, and some economists prefer measures of the community's wealth. Theoretical and statistical studies suggest that there may be economies of scale in the demand for real cash balances. That is, a one-percent increase in real income may result in somewhat less than a one-percent increase in m^D.[†]

Because m^D is not a constant, but responds to income and interest rates, a constant money supply does not lead to a constant price level. On the contrary, if the money supply M^S were constant, we would ordinarily expect prices to fall as m^D rises with real income. There may be additional fluctuations in prices due to interest rate changes. The most interesting cases (which we will discuss in Chapters 4 and 5) arise when these interest rate fluctuations are due to changing inflationary expectations.

We may summarize the demand for real cash balances in a diagram

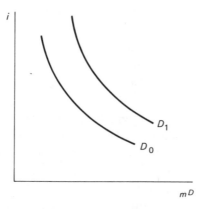

Fig. 2-3. Demand for real cash balances.

[†]If the M_2 definition of money is used (see footnote, p. 17), a one-percent increase in real income seems to cause almost a two-percent increase in m^D, at least historically. However, it is not clear whether this can be expected to continue as real income grows further, or if it is simply due to institutional changes favoring time deposits in the last few decades.

like Fig. 2-3. Real cash balances m^D are on the horizontal axis, and the market interest rate i is on the vertical axis. D_0 is the demand for real cash balances for one level of transactions or real income. It slopes downward, since the higher the interest rate, the smaller the demand for m. D_1 is the demand curve for a higher level of transactions and real income. It lies to the right of D_0, since for a given interest rate more money will be desired the higher the level of income.

THE SPEED OF ADJUSTMENT

Some of the more extreme 18th century adherents of the "quantity theory" actually believed that if a gold coin were placed under each person's pillow one night, the next morning prices would be proportionately higher. Surely this is a slight exaggeration of the adjustment process. Extra dollars linger in your wallet or checkbook for days, weeks, or even months at a time before their presence is noticed by anyone else in the marketplace. Even then this first-round effect pulls prices only a small fraction of the way to their new equilibrium level. Each subsequent round also takes time.

The process is further slowed by the fact that an inflationary or deflationary change in the money supply may temporarily move real income and interest rates in the direction required to change m^D so as to lessen the disequilibrium. For example, a sudden decrease in the money supply should start prices moving downward. However (as we will see in Chapter 6), this deflation may cause unemployment to rise and income to fall temporarily. This reduced income will tend to bring m^D down, reducing the gap between m^D and M^S/P and slowing the deflation. We would expect a sudden increase in the money supply to have the opposite effect, which will be damped by a temporary rise in income and m^D.

Furthermore, an increase in the money supply through the banking system comes about as the banks make loans at lower interest rates than would otherwise prevail. These lower interest rates act to increase m^D, again reducing the gap between m^D and M^S/P and slowing the inflation.

Likewise, a bank contraction reduces M^S at the same time it drives interest rates up and m^D down.

Just how long this adjustment should take is difficult to say, either theoretically or on the basis of statistical evidence. However, one recent study suggests that it takes about 6 months for the process to go halfway to completion, another 6 months to go half of the remaining way, and so on.[†] This estimate seems reasonable, in terms of the probable size of the price changes in each round and the time likely to elapse between successive rounds of price adjustments.

REFERENCES

An excellent description of the inflationary process as an injection of new money works its way into the economy is contained in Ludwig von Mises, *The Theory of Money and Credit* (New Haven, Connecticut: Yale Univ. Press, 1953), pp. 108–153.

Walras' law is so called because it was discovered by John Stuart Mill long before Walras' time. See "Of the Influence of Consumption on Production" in Mill's *Essays on Some Unsettled Questions of Political Economy* (originally 1844, reprinted 1948, Aldwych, London). The fact that Walras' law wasn't discovered by Walras is an application of Stigler's law, which states that no economic law is named for its actual discoverer. Enigma: Who discovered Stigler's law?) An elaborate discussion of the interaction of money, income, interest rates, and prices using Walras' law is contained in Don Patinkin's *Money, Interest, and Prices* (New York: Harper & Row, 1965), 2nd edition, Chapters 9–12. Walras' law has come under fire in an important, though I believe mistaken, article by Robert W. Clower, "The Keynesian Counterrevolution: A Theoretical Appraisal," In F.H. Hahn and F.P.R. Brechling, editors, *The Theory of Interest Rates* (London: St. Martin's, 1965).

A superbly simple mathematical model of the demand for money is described by William Baumol, "The Transactions Demand for Cash: An Inventory Theoretic Approach," *The Quarterly Journal of Economics* (November, 1952).

[†] Stephen M. Goldfeld, "The Demand for Money Revisited," *Brookings Papers on Economic Activity* (1973), pp. 577–646.

Terms to Remember

WPI
CPI
GNP deflator
Real cash balances
Nominal cash balances
Walras' law
Quantity theory of money

VELOCITY AND
THE QUANTITY EQUATION

One way of organizing concepts about the relation between money, income, and prices is through the "quantity equation," which relates these quantities to the "velocity" of money.

TRANSACTIONS VELOCITY

In Chapter 1, the demand for real cash balances arises because people have to receive money before they spend it. For all practical purposes this means that they have to hang on to it for at least a little while. If we knew how long on average people kept each unit of money before spending it, as well as the total real volume of transactions, we would be able to compute the demand for real cash balances.

For example, suppose people tended to hold on to each dollar for one week or one fifty-second of a year on average. Taking 1967 as the base year for our price index, assume that during this year 10.4 trillion 1967 dollars' worth of transactions take place. Then the demand for real cash balances would be $10.4/52 = 0.2$ trillion or 200 billion 1967 dollars.[†] If the supply of nominal cash balances were actually 300 billion dollars, this year's price index would have to be 1.50 in order to equate the supply and demand for money.

If people hold on to each dollar one week on average, that means that the average dollar changes hands once a week, or 52 times per year. This rate at which dollars change hands is called the *transactions velocity of money.* [‡]

Let V_t be the transactions velocity of money and t the real value of the transactions that take place in one year. Then, as in our illustration above, the demand for real cash balances will be given by

$$m^D = \frac{t}{V_t} \qquad (3\text{-}1)$$

In equilibrium, when supply equals demand, this expression times P just equals the supply of nominal cash balances:

$$M^S = \frac{Pt}{V_t} \qquad (3\text{-}2)$$

If we rearrange Eq. (3-2) and substitute M for M^S (since the nominal money supply is just the number of dollars in existence), we obtain the *transactions version* of the quantity equation:

$$\boxed{MV_t = Pt} \qquad (3\text{-}3)$$

The quantity equation can be looked upon as merely defining the velocity of money:

[†]Note to British readers: In the U.S., a "trillion' is a thousand billions rather than a million billions. A "billion" is the same as a milliard (a thousand millions), instead of a million millions.

[‡]"Frequency" might have been a more appropriate name for this concept than "velocity." Nevertheless, it was originally called velocity, and that name has stuck.

$$V_t = \frac{Pt}{M} \qquad (3\text{-}4)$$

From this point of view, the quantity equation is as indisputable as any definition. But the quantity theory gives it greater significance by regarding it as the relation by which the nominal money supply together with velocity and real transactions determine the price level:

$$P = \frac{MV_t}{t} \qquad (3\text{-}5)$$

Looking at the quantity equation in this manner, as determining the price level, assumes (a) that demand and supply for money are roughly in equilibrium, (b) that the demand for real cash balances is determined by the average length of time people plan to hold each dollar, and (c) that this time is roughly independent of P, M, and t.

Of course, each dollar doesn't have exactly the same "velocity." Some people spend or invest money as fast as they receive it, giving their dollars a very high V_t. Others may hang on to money for months or even years, giving their dollars a low V_t. If the relative importance in the economy of these two types of people changes, there will be a change in the economy's average V_t.

Velocity is also sensitive to interest rates. If interest rates are high, velocity will be high, because people will want to get their dollars invested as soon as possible if they aren't going to spend them. Likewise, if interest rates are low, velocity will be low. This is just another way of expressing the negative relation between m^D and interest rates that we discussed in Chapter 2, because m^D is inversely proportional to velocity. [See Eq. (3-1).]

Measured velocity might also fluctuate if the demand and supply of money are out of equilibrium. If people are suddenly given extra money, prices will not change immediately, so people's nominal rate of spending Pt will not rise in proportion to the change in M. According to Eq. (3-4), this means that V_t must fall. This makes sense, since if people don't increase their spending in the same proportion as their cash balances have gone up, they must retain some of the dollars longer. As prices rise, however, V_t will go back up.

Income Velocity

In practice, we do not know what the rate of transactions is. It is easier to find statistics on income, if only because net income is more important for tax purposes. Therefore, real income y[†] is ordinarily used in place of real transactions t in the quantity equation. When this is done, "income velocity" V replaces transactions velocity V_t:

$$V = \frac{Py}{M} \tag{3-6}$$

[Compare Eq. (3-4).] When we refer just to "velocity," we mean income velocity, rather than transactions velocity. As long as transactions are roughly proportional to income, income velocity and real income will be just as useful as determinants of the demand for real cash balances as are transactions velocity and real transactions.

Transactions velocity is always greater than income velocity, simply because the total of transactions always exceeds net income. To illustrate this, suppose a farmer sells wheat to a miller for $50, and let us assume this is all income to the farmer. The miller sells the flour he grinds to a baker for $80, adding $80 to transactions, but only $80 − $50 = $30 to income. The baker sells the bread he bakes to consumers for $100, adding only $20 to income. Total transactions are $50 + $80 + $100 = $230, while total income is only $50 + $30 + $20 = $100. The reason income is smaller is that while each item of income arises in a transaction, only part of the transaction is income, while the rest represents costs.

To give an idea of the relative size of income and transactions velocity in the United States, the nominal money supply was about a quarter of national income in 1973, so that income velocity was about 4.0 per year. Transactions velocity is harder to measure, but some indication of its magnitude is given by the fact that demand deposits turned over at a rate of about 60 times per year outside New York City. That is, the sum of all

---

[†] Real income is ordinary nominal income expressed in current dollars, divided by the price index. It therefore expresses units of purchasing power in terms of the base year for the price index. As with cash balances and transactions, we use a lowercase letter to represent this real quantity. Nominal income then equals Py.

checks written on these accounts was approximately 60 times the average value of the sum of the balances in these accounts. If currency and deposits in New York City turned over at this rate as well, transactions velocity would equal 60.0 per year, far greater than income velocity.

If we multiply both sides of Eq. (3-6) by M, we get the *income version* of the quantity equation:

$$MV = Py$$ (3-7)

Old-fashioned "quantity theorists" held that velocity is a constant determined by the financial habits of the public, so that for a given level of real income, prices would be directly proportional to the nominal money supply, and the adjustment would be instantaneous. The quantity theory fell out of fashion with the rise of Keynesian economics during the 1930s. But in the last two decades it has come back to life, partly due to the efforts of Milton Friedman of the University of Chicago, and partly because of the growing worry about inflation. Although modern "monetarists" often couch their monetary theory in terms of the quantity equation, they are willing to admit that in the short run, an increase or decrease in the money supply is liable to be absorbed by a corresponding increase or decrease in real income or by a decrease or increase in velocity, rather than by a rise in prices. (If P and y are constant and M goes up, V must fall by definition.) Furthermore, it is now recognized that even in the long run, the equilibrium rate of velocity is likely to be affected by interest rates, and possibly even the level of real income, as well as undergoing shifts due to innovations in the technology of making payments, such as computerized credit card transactions. Nevertheless, this revival of interest in the quantity theory has again focused attention on the long-run relation between the money supply and the price level.

DIFFERENCE FORM OF THE QUANTITY EQUATION

The quantity equation relates the *levels* of money, velocity, prices, and income to one another. What does it imply about percentage changes in these values?

Suppose that M, V, P, and y change by ΔM, ΔV, ΔP, and Δy. The quantity equation must hold after these changes have occurred, so we may substitute $M + \Delta M$, $V + \Delta V$, etc., into (3-7):

$$(M + \Delta M)(V + \Delta V) = (P + \Delta P)(y + \Delta y) \tag{3-8}$$

Expanding the products gives us four terms on each side:

$$MV + V \Delta M + M \Delta V + \Delta M \Delta V = Py + y \Delta P + P \Delta y + \Delta P \Delta y \tag{3-9}$$

Now MV still equals Py, so we may divide the left side by MV and the right side by Py and still maintain equality:

$$1 + \frac{\Delta M}{M} + \frac{\Delta V}{V} + \frac{\Delta M}{M} \frac{\Delta V}{V} = 1 + \frac{\Delta P}{P} + \frac{\Delta y}{y} + \frac{\Delta P}{P} \frac{\Delta y}{y} \tag{3-10}$$

We may subtract the 1 from both sides and still have equality. Furthermore, so long as the change in our variables is only a few percent per time period, the last term on each side may be dropped without seriously affecting the equality, since it will be much smaller than the other terms. This leaves us with the *difference form* of the quantity equation:

$$\boxed{\frac{\Delta M}{M} + \frac{\Delta V}{V} = \frac{\Delta P}{P} + \frac{\Delta y}{y}} \tag{3-11}$$

This equation looks a lot like the original quantity equation, except that it adds percentage changes instead of multiplying levels.[†]

Let us try an example. Suppose that the money supply grows by 5%, while real income only grows by 3%, and velocity remains constant. What will be the rate of growth of prices? We may solve the difference form of the quantity equation for $\Delta P/P$ to get

$$\begin{aligned}
\frac{\Delta P}{P} &= \frac{\Delta M}{M} + \frac{\Delta V}{V} - \frac{\Delta y}{y} \\
&= (0.05) + (0.00) - (0.03) \\
&= 0.02
\end{aligned} \tag{3-12}$$

or 2% inflation.

[†] Students who have had calculus will realize that if instantaneous rates of change are used instead of discrete changes, Eq. (3-11) holds exactly instead of only approximately.

One important implication of our equation is that if velocity is constant, the rate of change of the money supply just necessary to keep prices constant is equal to the rate of growth of real income. Of course, velocity isn't always constant. Probably the primary immediate effect of an unusual excess of $\Delta M/M$ over $\Delta y/y$ is a reduction of V, rather than an increase in P. Even in the long run, velocity may change permanently due to changes in the interest rate or other factors. However, these factors that change velocity are (with the exception of expected inflation, which we will discuss in Chapter 4) hard to predict. Therefore, a policy of letting the nominal money supply grow at the long-run trend rate of growth of real income (3 or 4% per year) may be the best that is humanly possible to provide price stability.

[*Note:* The following problems require solving Eq. (3-11) for $\Delta V/V$ and other rates of change. The student should become proficient at rearranging (3-11) to solve for any of its terms.]

Problem 3-1

If income is growing at the annual rate of 4% and the money supply is growing at the annual rate of 6%, what must be the change in velocity if prices only go up by 1%?

Problem 3-2

What monetary growth rate is required to maintain price stability ($\Delta P/P = 0$) if real income is expected to grow by 5% and velocity is expected to fall by 3%?

Problem 3-3

If the nominal money supply grows by 8%, prices rise by 6%, and velocity rises by 1%, what must have happened to real income?

NONMONETARY CAUSES OF INFLATION

How can the relation between the demand and supply of money determine the price level, independently of other forces in the economy that drive prices up?

If important sectors of the economy are monopolized by firms or unions that are protected from competition, won't they demand ever higher and higher prices and wages, leading to inflation whether there is monetary expansion or not? The answer is no, because it is not to the advantage of a monopolist to charge an arbitrarily high price. He finds a price at which his profits are maximized, and the price he charges will be higher than the price that would prevail if his market were subject to competitive pressures. But at any higher price, the quantity he can sell falls off so fast that his profits would be smaller. A monopolist charges *high* prices, but not *rising* prices. Similarly, a union that prevents competition from outsiders gets *high* wages, but not *rising* wages. It is true that a *growing degree of monopoly power* will imply *rising* prices for the monopolized goods. However, it is not clear what effect this would have on the overall price level, since the consumers who must buy the monopolized goods will have less left over to spend on other goods. If the prices of other goods fall, the general price level may remain constant or even fall.

There *is* a way that a growing degree of monopolization could raise the price level, but that is through the demand for money. Monopoly pricing, whether by firms or unions, reduces the overall efficiency of production and therefore lowers real income below what it otherwise would be. Thus *growing* monopolization may reduce the *rate of growth* of real income, and through the quantity equation make prices grow more than they otherwise would for any given rate of growth of M (assuming the monopolization has no effect on velocity).

What about the famous wage–price spiral? Couldn't an initial rise in wages, for whatever reason, lead to a rise in the cost of production and therefore in the prices of consumer goods, and wouldn't this rise in the cost of living lead to a further rise in wage demands, resulting in an endless spiral of inflation? This might happen for a round or two. However, if the rise in prices were not validated by a comparable increase in the money supply, real cash balances would fall to less than the demand for them. By Walras' law, this excess demand for m would imply a corresponding excess supply for other goods in general. This growing excess supply would exert an ever more powerful downward pull on prices, until the wage–

price spiral were halted or even reversed.† Another way of looking at this process is that if *P* rises of its own accord, the purchasing power of people who hold money falls, just as if prices were constant but you took money away from them and burned it. This reduction in their real wealth (known as the real balance effect) leads them to try to reduce their standard of living slightly, pulling *P* back down until the equilibrium price level is restored.

SUPPRESSED INFLATION

Couldn't price ceilings keep the price level from rising even though the money supply were increasing faster than the demand for money? Yes and no. We calculate the price index in order to estimate changes in the value of money. Money has a certain value because we know we can get things in exchange for it at certain prices. There are two ways it can lose this value: if the prices go up, or if we can no longer get things in exchange for it at constant prices.

Controls (if enforced) can keep prices and therefore the price index from rising, in spite of inflationary increases in the money supply. But they cannot guarantee that you can buy anything at those prices. When the value of money is falling but price controls keep this depreciation from showing up in recorded prices, there is said to be *suppressed inflation*.

Everyone remembers the dramatic consequences of price controls in the winter of 1973-74. Late in 1973, gas was about a third of a dollar per gallon, with local variations. The Arab oil embargo, on top of general inflationary pressures, raised the market clearing price to perhaps half a

---

†This sort of effect is consistent with data on inflation in Chile, according to a recent Boston College Ph.D. dissertation by Susan Wachter. In the short run (one or two quarters), the price index is sensitive to shifts in demand between sectors, but in the longer run, the money supply takes over.

dollar per gallon. The Office of the Energy Czar[†] decided to get tough and prevent this rise, or at least delay it. It was successful in keeping the price lower than it would have been, but with one hitch—you had the greatest difficulty finding any gas to buy. Without the controls, one dollar could have bought two gallons. With the controls, one dollar could *not* buy three gallons (or could buy three gallons, but only with the added cost of a long search and wait in line). Obviously a dollar that can buy only two gallons is worth less than one that can buy three. However, it is not clear which dollar is worth less, the one that can buy two gallons or the one that *can't* buy three. Many people demonstrated that they regarded the latter as worth less, by jumping at the opportunity to pay a full dollar a gallon at one station in Brooklyn. (Its owner was quickly prosecuted for this "disservice.") Without controls, if every station had tried to raise its price to a dollar a gallon, they would all have been very short on customers. Competition between them for customers would quickly have driven the price down towards 50¢ per gallon. The one service station that did charge a dollar was able to do a good business only because most of the others were intimidated into respecting the ceilings. Consequently, it got the overflow from a very large market.

Those who have actually worked in price control agencies often look back with favor on how the system operates. For instance, John Kenneth Galbraith, who was Deputy Administrator in the World War II Office of Price Administration (OPA) from 1941 to 1943, has been one of the most outspoken advocates of price controls. If these controls just cause shortages, why would anyone with intimate knowledge of them be in favor? The answer is that when market prices are not allowed to allocate resources, someone has to take over and say which buyers may buy at the low controlled prices and which buyers must go empty-handed. The government, often in the person of the price administrator himself, ends up with this job.[‡] The price administrator finds himself in control of the

---

[†] Alias Office of Energy Administration, alias Federal Energy Administration.

[‡] As Galbraith points out, "A market system in which wages and prices are set by the state is a market system no more. Only the blithely obtuse can reconcile 'this Free Enterprise System' with the enforcement of wage and price controls." *Economics and the Public Order* (Boston: Houghton Mifflin, 1973), p. 312.

welfare and destiny of millions. The vignette on p. 40 is only a slight exaggeration of a day in the life of the price controller.

In his private life as a university professor (Galbraith) or as a pillar of Wall Street (pipe-smoking William Simon), the controller has only limited power over students or customers, since they retain the option of enrolling in a different course or taking their accounts to another firm. But as price controller, people have to go along with his rulings or do without. In this role, everyone the price controller comes into contact with at last appreciates what he knows to be his true importance. It is no wonder he tends to have a glowing recollection of how the price control system works.

If controls are not effective or are not enforced, they are harmless, but then they might as well not exist. Gradually through the first quarter of 1974 the price control people allowed stations to raise their prices. When the ceiling passed the market clearing price, the controls became ineffective and the lines disappeared. On the other hand, if the official price had been set at a low effective level like 1¢ per gallon, but this ceiling had not been enforced with prosecutions, once again the ceiling would have been harmless. It should therefore be kept in mind when looking for the adverse effects of price controls that before these effects appear, the controls must be both effective *and* enforced.

The shortages caused by price ceilings that *are* effective and enforced mean that money can no longer be used to buy goods freely at the controlled price. Therefore, ceilings cannot keep the value of money from falling. They can keep the price index from rising, since the index is sure to be computed from the controlled prices. But to the extent that they have any effect at all (as evidenced by the shortages they cause), such a price index becomes increasingly meaningless with regard to the purpose for which we calculate it.

Some form of price controls existed from August, 1971 to April, 1974.[†] Toward the end of this period, the CPI probably greatly understated the deterioration of the value of money that had occurred since 1971. From August, 1971 to January, 1973, it only reported a 3.2% annual inflation rate. As the controls started to be removed, the CPI began to record realistically inflation that in fact had already occurred, but that had been suppressed. Thus, the 8.8% rise reported for 1973 and the 12.2% rise reported for 1974 were at least partially the belated recognition of the

[†]Power to control oil prices continued even after April, 1974.

Price controls: January, 1974 (copyright, 1974, G.B. Trudeau; distributed by Universal Press Syndicate).

full magnitude of the fall in the dollar's purchasing power during 1971 and 1972.

World War II is another good example of suppressed inflation. The money supply more than doubled from 1941 to 1945, but thanks to the OPA, prices only went up by 22%. During the war, goods were not freely available at the official prices. Especially underpriced goods like meat, tires, and gasoline could only be had with ration coupons or on the illegal black market. When the wartime controls were removed, the suppressed inflation emerged. By 1948, prices were already 63% above their 1941 level.

Price controls are usually accompanied by demands for price rollbacks that would change the prices for transactions that have already taken place. Rollbacks (illustrated on p. 42) are as futile as price controls as a means of stemming inflation, but they have appeal to politicians in that they present an opportunity to transfer purchasing power from harried businesses to political insiders or pressure groups who have made significant purchases.

SUPPRESSED DEFLATION

Incredible though it may seem to the modern generation, from time to time prices actually fall instead of rising. In the first few years of the Great Depression of the 1930s, for instance, prices fell at an annual rate of 7%, as a result of the massive contraction of bank credit that accompanied the onset of the depression. Rather than let prices and wages adjust quickly to the shrunken money supply, the government tried to halt the deflation with price and wage *floors*. A floor is just like a ceiling, only upside down. With a ceiling, you have a very hard time finding anyone to *sell* to you at the controlled price. Demand exceeds supply, and queues of buyers start to form. Store shelves go bare. With a floor, you have an equally hard time finding anyone to *buy* from you at the controlled price. Supply exceeds demand, and queues of unsold inventories and unemployed workers begin to form. Store aisles go bare. Output remains unsold while workers and factories are idled.

Price rollbacks *(by permission of John Hart and Field Enterprises, Inc.).*

It is instructive to compare the experience of the thirties with that of the depression of 1921-22. In the earlier depression, prices and wages were slashed wherever excess supply appeared. Soon recovery was in sight, and unemployment was down to reasonable levels. In the thirties, on the other hand, the government made every effort to resist the deflation. Already in 1929, President Hoover was imploring business leaders to keep wages up, with considerable success. In 1931, one misguided economist jubilantly observed "it is indeed impossible to recall any past depression of similar intensity and duration in which the wages of prosperity were maintained as long as they have been during the depression of 1930-31."[†] As one would expect, unemployment (unsold labor services) got worse and worse instead of going away. Hoover's jawbone techniques for persuading firms to keep wages up voluntarily eventually began to lose their effect, but under Roosevelt they were soon replaced by compulsory wage and price floors administered by an agency misleadingly named the National Recovery Administration (NRA).[‡] These and other efforts to suppress the deflation required by the monetary contraction helped keep unemployment and excess supply of output at depression levels throughout the decade.

REFERENCES

Friedman's essay "The Quantity Theory of Money—A Restatement" is usually cited as the source of recent interest in the quantity theory. It appears in *Studies in the Quantity Theory of Money*, a book edited by Friedman (Chicago, Illinois: Univ. of Chicago Press, 1956). See also Irving Fisher's *The Purchasing Power of Money* (originally published in 1911; reprinted, New York: Kelley, 1965). The Keynes of the *Treatise on Money* (New York: Harcourt Brace, 1957; originally published in 1930) was much

---

[†] Leo Wolman, quoted in Murray Rothbard, *America's Great Depression* (Princeton, New Jersey: Van Nostrand, 1963), p. 237. Chapters 7-12 of Rothbard's book are an important revisionist interpretation of the Hoover administration.

[‡] This was before truth-in-packaging, which in any event doesn't apply to Congress.

less "Keynesian" and more "monetarist" than the Keynes of the *General Theory of Employment, Interest, and Money* (New York: Harcourt Brace, 1957; originally published in 1936).

Terms to Remember

Quantity theory of money
Quantity equation
Transactions velocity
Income velocity
Suppressed inflation
OPA
Suppressed deflation
NRA

EXPECTED INFLATION AND INTEREST RATES

REAL VERSUS NOMINAL INTEREST RATES

If you lend money for a year at 10% interest, but during that year prices rise by 7%, the purchasing power of your savings will have grown by only 3%. This rate is your *realized real interest rate*. You would have done as well to have lent your money out at only 3% during a period of constant prices.

In real life, you can only guess what the inflation rate is going to be. This *expected inflation rate*, together with the agreed-upon *nominal interest rate* of the loan (10% in the above example), determines the *expected real interest rate*. When people decide to lend money at a certain interest rate, they take into account how much extra real consumption they expect to be able to get in the future in exchange for forgoing some consumption in the present, so it is the expected real interest rate that governs people's savings decisions. Similarly, when firms borrow money to finance production, what matters is not the nominal interest rate, but the expected real interest rate. If prices (including the prices of their products) all go up, they can afford to pay back that many more dollars than they could have if prices had been constant.

The expected real interest rate does not necessarily equal the realized real interest rate, because people seldom anticipate inflation correctly. In the above example, if you had been expecting only 6% inflation, and lent your money out at 10%, the expected real interest rate would have been 4%, not 3%. Four percent would have been the figure influencing you to lend this money out instead of increasing your consumption. The three-percent figure had no effect on your behavior, because you had no way of foreseeing that that is what your real rate of return was actually going to be.

Since it is the expected real interest rate that affects lending and borrowing behavior, rather than the realized real interest rate, economists often single out the former as *the* real interest rate. Consumption tastes and production technology determine the (expected) real interest rate pretty much independently of expected inflation.[†] Therefore, if we compare two states of the world with the same tastes and technology but different expected inflation rates, the real interest rates will be virtually identical, while the nominal interest rates will differ by the difference between the expected inflation rates.

We will denote the (expected) real interest rate by the letter r, and the nominal interest rate that is written into the loan contract by the letter i. We have already used $\Delta P/P$ to represent the actual rate of inflation. We will use this same expression, with an asterisk attached, to represent the anticipated inflation rate:

$$(\Delta P/P)^* = \text{anticipated inflation rate}$$

[†] See Irving Fisher, *The Theory of Interest* (New York: Kelley, 1965; originally published in 1930).

The real interest rate is equal to the nominal interest rate minus the expected inflation rate:

$$r = i - (\Delta P/P)^* \qquad (4\text{-}1)$$

Equivalently, the nominal interest rate is the sum of the real rate and the expected inflation rate. Also, the expected inflation rate is the difference between the nominal rate and the real rate:

$$i = r + (\Delta P/P)^* \qquad (4\text{-}2)$$

$$(\Delta P/P)^* = i - r \qquad (4\text{-}3)$$

Problem 4-1

(a) If r is 6% per annum, while i is 4% per annum, what is the expected inflation rate?

(b) If people instead expected 3% inflation, what would i and r be?

GIBSON'S PARADOX

Around the turn of the century, an English statistician named Gibson observed the following paradox: As the banks increase the money supply, one would think that they would drive prices up because of the quantity theory. At the same time, one would think that their loan expansion would drive interest rates down. Gibson therefore expected to see the highest price levels coinciding with the lowest interest rates and the lowest price levels coinciding with the highest interest rates. Yet when he looked at actual price and interest rate data for the nineteenth century, he observed just the opposite: The highest values of the price level coincided with the highest values of interest rates, and vice versa.

Graphically, what Gibson expected to see was something like the graphs of P and i in Fig. 4-1. What he actually saw looked more like Fig. 4-2.

Fig. 4-1. What Gibson expected to see.

Gibson's paradox was later solved by the famous Yale economist, Irving Fisher. Fisher pointed out that what Gibson was observing was the nominal interest rate, rather than the real interest rate. After a long period of inflationary monetary expansion, when prices are at their highest levels, people will have come to expect further inflation. This means that the nominal interest rate will exceed the real interest rate. Although the bank expansion may have the effect of lowering the real interest rate somewhat, the increase in inflationary expectations is liable to completely offset this effect, so that nominal interest rates will actually be at their highest. This means that a peak in the price level should actually correspond to a peak in the nominal interest rate.

Similarly, a prolonged period of deflationary monetary contraction (or a deflationary constant money supply during a period of real growth)

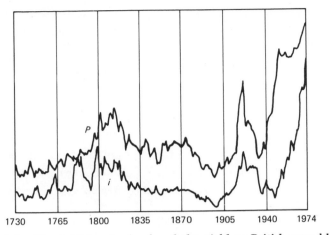

1730   1765   1800   1835   1870   1905   1940   1974

Fig. 4-2. The British price level and the yield on British consol bonds.
Reprinted with permission from Robert Shiller and Jeremy Siegel, "The Gibson Paradox and Expected Real Rates of Interest" (unpublished paper, 1975). Shiller and Siegel present alternatives to Fisher's classic resolution of Gibson's paradox. Figure 4-1 is the same as 4-2, with the i-series inverted. The price level is plotted on a logarithmic scale.

will result in *deflationary* expectations when the price level is at its minimum. This implies that the troughs in the price level will coincide with the troughs in nominal interest rates.

The phenomenon that Gibson observed, given Fisher's explanation, has an important implication for the formation of the expected inflation rate. It indicates that to a large degree expected inflation is based on the experience of inflation in the moderately recent past.

Another implication has to do with the effect of monetary expansion on interest rates. In the short run, a higher rate of monetary expansion will probably reduce the interest rate, whether through the direct effect of bank expansion on the loan market, or through the "liquidity" effect of the temporary excess supply of money (see Chapter 2, p. 23). However, the monetary expansion will increase the inflation rate. In the long run, inflationary expectations will catch up with actual inflation, and the nominal interest rate (which is the one that is observed) will end up higher than it started. A recent statistical study found that a sustained increase in the rate of monetary growth makes interest rates lower and lower, but only for about 6 to 8 months. Then they start to come back up again. After 12 to 18 months, they pass their original level, and continue to climb.[†]

EXPECTED INFLATION AND VELOCITY

In the previous chapters, we noted that the demand for money, and therefore velocity, is sensitive to the interest rate. As shown in Fig. 2-3, m^D should decline with interest rates. Equation (3-6) may be rewritten using the relation between real and nominal cash balances, $m = M/P$, as

$$V = \frac{y}{m} \tag{4-4}$$

If the supply and demand for money are in equilibrium, and assuming that y is relatively constant, this equation implies that velocity will increase with interest rates.

The interest rate that is relevant to the demand for money (and therefore to velocity) is the nominal interest rate, rather than the real interest rate. This can be rationalized either in nominal terms or in real terms. In nominal terms, if you hold money, you get a zero nominal rate of return.[‡] If you hold bonds, you receive i percent each year. The difference is i percent. In real terms, if you hold money, you will lose (or at least believe you will lose) purchasing power equal to the expected in-

---

[†]Phillip Cagan and Arthur Gandolfi, "The Lag in Monetary Policy as Implied by the Time Pattern of Monetary Effects on Interest Rates," *American Economic Review* (May, 1969), pp. 277–284.

[‡]In this book, we assume that demand deposits (checking accounts) earn no interest. This has been true throughout the United States from 1933 up until recently. In the last couple of years, court decisions and special legislation have allowed people in Massachusetts and New Hampshire to earn interest on their checking accounts. Of course, everyone in the United Sates is equal before the law. However, in Orwellian fashion, the citizens of these two states are just a little *more* equal than the citizens of other states.

flation rate $(\Delta P/P)^*$ times the sum in question. If you hold bonds, you believe you will come out ahead by the expected real interest rate r. The difference, according to Eq. (4-2), is just the nominal interest rate i. Either way, the opportunity cost of holding money is the nominal interest rate.

The real interest rate does fluctuate, but it is seldom outside a relatively small range—my guess is 2-5% for long-term rates. However, the inflation rate (and therefore the expected inflation rate) can be almost anything. In this century, we have had years with 17% inflation (during World War I), and years with 11% deflation (right after World War I). By world standards, this record made us look like a country with a relatively *stable* price level. Since inflation, and therefore inflationary expectations, can take on a very wide range of values, we may expect the most important fluctuations in the nominal interest rate to be those brought about by changes in expected inflation, rather than by changes in the real interest rate.

Through their impact on the nominal interest rate, high inflationary expectations mean small m^D and a high level of velocity. In other words, people will try to get rid of their money—spend it on goods that at least will retain a constant real value—before it loses its purchasing power. This is sometimes known as the Jeff Effect (see p. 52). Similarly, low inflationary expectations means large m^D and a low level of velocity.

In this book, we assume for the sake of simplicity that the economy has a smoothly operating capital market, so that the opportunity cost of holding money (in nominal terms) is the nominal interest rate. However, governmental interference with the capital market might prevent observed nominal interest rates from fully reflecting inflationary expectations. The maximum interest rate allowed by law might even reflect a negative real rate of return. What then? In this case, a zero real rate of return could still be obtained by hoarding consumer goods. For example, next month's canned goods could be purchased this month instead of next month, giving a nominal rate of return equal to the expected rise in the price of canned soup, interest ceiling or not. The official nominal interest rate would simply be ignored, and the demand for money would still respond to inflationary expectations. Savings would be diverted from productive invest-

High inflationary expectations cause high velocity (*reprinted with permission from The McNaught Syndicate, Inc.*).

ment to unproductive hoarding, but that is a different problem we don't
have time for here.

RECENT EXPERIENCE

Rising inflationary expectations cause *rising* velocity, which means
that we must take the $\Delta V/V$ term into account in the quantity equation.
When we solve the quantity equation for the inflation rate as in Eq. (3-12),
we see that rising velocity makes inflation even greater than it otherwise
would be, given the rates of growth of the nominal money stock and real
income. Conversely, falling inflationary expectations lead to falling velocity, and tend to be *de*flationary. The former case is illustrated by recent
experience in the United States.

Over the ten-year period from 1964 to 1974, monetary growth averaged 5.9% per year. Real income grew at a rate of 3.5% per year, and
inflation averaged 5.2% per year. Clearly, inflation was greater than the
excess of the growth in M over the growth in y. Does this experience
contradict the quantity theory?

No, because this was almost certainly a period of rising inflationary
expectations. Over the previous ten-year period, the nominal money supply grew by only 2.0% per year. A somewhat more inflationary monetary
growth rate during the Viet Nam period and afterwards led to higher
inflation, and *rising* inflationary expectations. In addition to the 2.4%
inflation that would have occurred with constant velocity, the rise in
inflationary expectations apparently induced a 2.8% per year increase in
velocity, itself the indirect result of monetary expansion. Evidence of the
rise in inflationary expectations is provided by the nominal interest rate on
high-grade corporate bonds, which rose from 4.4% in 1964 to 8.7% in
1974.[†]

SELF-GENERATING INFLATION

This feedback from inflationary expectations to the inflation rate
itself raises a disturbing possibility: A small amount of inflation, due per-

[†]Data from *The Economic Report of the President* and the Federal Reserve Bank of St. Louis.

haps to a slight discrepancy between the rate of growth of real income and that of the money supply, could lead to rising inflationary expectations and rising nominal interest rates. This in turn leads to a rise in velocity and further inflation. This inflation could cause a further rise in inflationary expectations, further growth in velocity, and yet more inflation even if $\Delta M/M$ remains roughly equal to $\Delta y/y$. A "noninflationary" monetary policy that lets the money supply grow at about the same rate as real income could result in runaway inflation. This possible vicious circle is illustrated in Fig. 4-3.

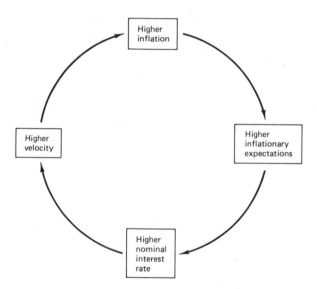

Fig. 4-3.   Self-generating inflation.

Equally conceivable is a self-generating *deflation*: An initial small amount of deflation could induce deflationary expectations, lowering the nominal interest rate. This could cause a decline in desired velocity, which would have an even further deflationary effect. This deflation could lead to even greater deflationary expectations, and so forth. The result would be a runaway deflation.

The possibility of self-generating inflation or deflation is one of the disadvantages of being on a fiat money standard. If the currency were based on gold (or silver) instead, this could not happen. As the price level rose, the price of gold in terms of other goods would fall. As gold became cheaper, more and more gold would be diverted from monetary uses into nonmonetary uses such as jewelry or industrial purposes. This decline in the supply of monetary gold would offset the rise in velocity and bring the inflation under control. If the price level fell instead, gold would become more expensive in terms of goods. This higher real price of gold would encourage exploitation of marginal gold ore deposits, increasing the total stock of gold as well as diverting already mined nonmonetary gold into the mint. This increase in the monetary gold supply would offset the fall in velocity and bring the deflation under control.

A commodity standard has the disadvantage that there is no reason to expect the stock of the monetary commodity to increase in anything like the right proportion to ensure price stability. The managers of a fiat currency may not be able to guess precisely what the real growth of the economy will be, but they probably could do better than the vagaries of gold discoveries.

Does the immunity of a metallic standard to self-generating inflation make up for the uncontrollability of the money stock? The answer to this question depends on the likelihood of a self-generating inflation occurring under a paper money standard.

A self-generating inflation depends on two factors: the speed with which expected inflation catches up with actual inflation, and the responsiveness of velocity to changes in the nominal interest rate. If expectations were very slow to adjust, a freak inflation one year would barely change inflationary expectations. If the money supply remained on an even keel in subsequent years, the inflation would not be repeated and there would be no reason for expected inflation to grow further. The link between higher inflation and higher expected inflation in Fig. 4-3 would be broken, and the vicious circle of self-generating inflation interrupted (Fig. 4-4).

On the other hand, if velocity (or equivalently the demand for real cash balances) were completely indifferent to the nominal interest rate, observed inflation wouldn't cause a rise in velocity even if the expected rate of future inflation adjusted instantly to the current rate of inflation. The link between higher interest rates and higher velocity would be broken, and the vicious circle again interrupted (Fig. 4-5).

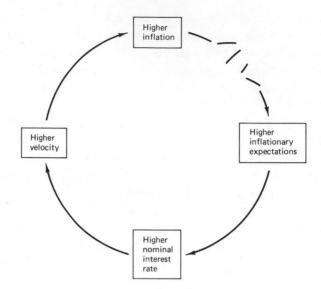

Fig. 4-4. Vicious circle broken by slow adjustment of inflationary expectations.

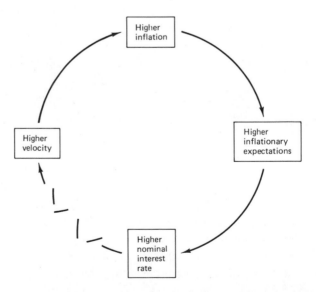

Fig. 4-5. Vicious circle broken by insensitivity of velocity to nominal interest rate.

The length of the lag in expectations and the interest-sensitivity of velocity have not been measured as accurately as we might wish in order to make a mathematical judgment of the possibility of self-generating inflation. However, no runaway inflation has ever occurred in history without simultaneous runaway increases in the money supply. Many instances of relatively stable fiat currencies are known. There are also many instances of high but steady inflation rates (on the order of 30% per year in some Latin American countries) accompanied by a comparably steady growth rate of the money supply. It therefore seems safe to say that self-generating inflation, while an interesting theoretical possibility, does not in fact occur. If we wish to explain runaway inflation we must look into the motives of the monetary authorities, in order to determine why they are sometimes led to increase the money supply at an ever-increasing rate. We discuss two of these motives in this chapter, a third in Chapter 5, and a fourth in Chapter 6.

LOW INTEREST RATE POLICY

In some political circles, it is felt that driving interest rates down should be the principal goal of monetary policy. For instance, in March of 1975, the House of Representatives passed a resolution, by an overwhelming vote of 367 to 55, urging the Federal Reserve System to dedicate its efforts to lowering long-term interest rates. This resolution doesn't have the force of law, but it does reflect a significant political sentiment. What would be the effect of this policy if it were seriously pursued?

With any given level of inflationary expectations and a monetary policy appropriate to maintaining an actual inflation rate equal to the given expected rate, the market's nominal interest rate would settle down to some level, which we will call the "equilibrium" interest rate. The short-run effect of monetary expansion, as we noted above, is to drive nominal interest rates down, below this equilibrium rate. With sufficiently rapid expansion, any target of low interest rates could be met. However, the rate at which the monetary authorities (in conjunction with the banking system) would have to increase the money supply increases with the difference between the target interest rate and the "equilibrium" interest rate. †As the policy proceeds, inflationary expectations will rise, and this

†This differs from Wicksell's natural rate by the expected inflation rate.

gap will widen. The low target interest rate will still be attainable, but only with faster monetary expansion, more rapid inflation, and an even wider gap between the equilibrium and target interest rates. In terms of the lags we discussed above in the section on Gibson's paradox, the short-run effect of monetary expansion is to lower interest rates, while the long-run effect is to raise nominal interest rates. The short-run effect can perpetually outweigh the long-run effect, but only provided the monetary expansion rate increases by leaps and bounds. In other words, the policy of pegging a low interest rate will lead to a runaway money supply (and therefore runaway inflation) if pursued with determination.

How far the runaway inflation goes and how fast it sets in depends on how low the target interest rate is (compared to the rate that would otherwise prevail), on the class of loans to which the policy is applied, and on the duration of the program. During World War II, for instance, the Federal Reserve System followed a policy of buying up all U.S. Government securities offered to it at high prices corresponding to fairly low interest rates. (These open-market operations directly create bank reserves, which can be used for expansion of the demand deposit component of the money supply.) The result was considerable inflation, most of which showed up at the end of the war as price controls were removed. However, there was certainly no hyperinflation *à la* Germany or Hungary (see Chapter 5), even though the policy was continued (with slightly higher target interest rates) up until the "Accord" of 1951.

One reason runaway inflation didn't set in under this policy is that interest rates probably wouldn't have been very high anyway. Throughout the depression years of the 1930s, market interest rates fell. On the eve of World War II, they were at extraordinarily low levels. We would expect the wartime demand to have driven up the equilibrium interest rate, but since it had such a lower level to rise from, it may not have needed to go very high.

In part it was due to the fact that the low target interest rates applied only to a limited class of securities. The lowest targets ($\frac{3}{8}$ of one percent!) applied only to 90-day Treasury bills, which were in limited supply. If a private citizen owned a Treasury bill, he could in effect borrow money at $\frac{3}{8}\%$ by selling his bill to the Fed. By the end of the war, however, the Fed had come to own virtually all the Treasury bills out-standing. There were practically none left in the hands of the public for the Fed to buy. The policy of buying bills at this rate could then have no further effect on the money supply. It would have been different if the Fed had been willing to discount any commercial paper at this rate, be-cause corporations can create IOU's *ad libitum*. The restriction on the kinds of debt whose interest rates the Fed tried to hold down put a limit on the inflationary potential of the fixed interest rate policy.

Since the Accord, the Fed has pursued a low interest rate policy to some extent, but without conviction. When the equilibrium interest rate was 3%, the Fed was inclined to push rates down towards 2%. When inflationary expectations raised the equilibrium rate to 5%, the Fed ad-justed its sights and tried for 4%. At 9%, the Fed was pushing for 8%. The irony of this policy is that if the monetary authorities would just forget about interest rates and let *M* grow at an annual rate of 3 or 4% come what may, interest rates would soon be back in the neighborhood of 2 to 5%.

If the Fed were to lend to all comers (or see to it that the banks were able to lend to all comers) at fixed low interest rates, the results would become explosive as the expected inflation rate passed the pegged interest rate. Then the expected real rate on bank loans would have be-come negative. It would pay to borrow from the banks just in order to store commodities in warehouses, for resale when the loan comes due. There would be no limit to the demand for such loans, and the money supply would increase as rapidly as clerical considerations permit.

According to the "passive accommodation doctrine," lowering the interest rate in this manner is harmless. The reasoning goes that as the banking system expands loans, new economic activity is made possible, which creates new demand for money. The increased demand for money just matches the increased supply, so the result is not inflationary. The banking system should just lie back and passively accommodate the de-mand of commerce for money.

The fallacy in the passive accommodation doctrine rests in the fact that firms that borrow money from the bank do not want money per se, but rather the factors of production—labor, materials, and so forth—that they can buy with it. The firm does not hold the additional money for the duration of the loan and then pay back the same dollars. Rather, it spends the money promptly, and repays the loan with the receipts from selling its product just before the loan is due. It is true that the extra transactions made possible by its ability to get the loan will increase its average cash balances a little, but this increase will be only a small fraction of the amount of the loan. Meanwhile, the money supply will have increased by the full amount of the loan. The increase in supply will be far greater than the increase in demand, and the net effect will be inflationary.

The "real bills doctrine" is one variant on the passive accommodation doctrine. According to this theory, passive accommodation is harmless only if it is restricted to high-grade, short-term, self-liquidating commercial loans. The banks should not base deposit creation on mortgages, long-term bonds, or consumer loans, but only on bills of exchange corresponding to real commercial transactions. It is true that banks following this prescription would be in a very sound position to meet runs against the deposits of individual banks. A concerted run on the whole banking system might cause temporary suspension of payments, but depositors could be paid very quickly, as these short-term loans were collected. But, however much this practice would contribute to bank liquidity, the inflationary implications of the bank expansion would remain.

THE REAL CASH BALANCES MIRAGE

An interesting argument tends to crop up during inflationary times. Its advocates observe that as inflation rises, real cash balances fall. They therefore argue that the monetary authorities, far from creating too much money, have actually created too *little* money. They go on to argue that the monetary authorities should get busy making the nominal money supply catch up with nominal income, so that real cash balances are restored to their original level, relative to real income. This is essentially the policy of the first two frames of the episode on p. 61.

The fallacy in this argument lies in its failure to recognize that in an inflation caused by excessive monetary expansion, we would expect

Idian monetary policy *(by permission of John Hart and Field Enterprises, Inc.).*

desired real cash balances to fall as inflationary expectations and nominal interest rates rise. Once an inflation is under way with excessive monetary expansion, real cash balances will be reduced to a lower level as prices are driven up by the increased supply of nominal cash balances and even further by the decreased demand for real balances. Measured real cash balances can *temporarily* be restored to their earlier level by even greater expansion of the nominal money supply, because monetary expansion causes prices to rise only with a lag in time. But eventually this greater expansion rate will cause prices to rise even faster, further lowering the equilibrium demand for real cash balances. To restore m to its original level now requires greater monetary expansion than ever. As the inflation rate rises higher and higher, the gap between real cash balances supplied and the equilibrium demand for real cash balances becomes larger and larger, so there will be no end to the growth of the monetary expansion and inflation rates. As with the passive accommodation doctrine, there will be a runaway money supply and a runaway inflation.

It is true that one of the real costs of inflation is that it forces individuals and firms to operate with smaller real cash balances than they would choose to employ without inflation. However, the monetary authorities cannot permanently restore real cash balances through additional monetary expansion. With every step they take in that direction, their goal will recede like a mirage in the desert. It is actually worse than a mirage; a mirage moves one step away from you with every step you take toward it. But the goal of restoring real cash balances to their preinflationary level recedes two steps with every step of monetary expansion. The only way to increase real cash balances permanently without runaway inflation is by *slowing* the rate of monetary expansion long enough for inflationary expectations to fall.

The King of Id's monetary program would not be worth mentioning if it were restricted to the funny pages. However, essentially the same proposal appears in the 1974 *Economic Report of the President* (pp. 31–32), where the Council of Economic Advisors, headed by Herbert Stein, projects 1% real growth and 7% inflation for the coming year and then recommends monetary growth of 8% in order to keep up with the two effects.[†] Stein was not delirious with Watergate fever—he was not implicated in that ruckus and hadn't been testifying under hot lights for hours on end. Nor is he a reckless innovator—he is generally respected as a cautious, middle-of-the-road economist. Rather, the appearance of this recommendation in the *Report* merely reflects the fact that all is not well with the state of cautious, middle-of-the-road economics, especially as regards its understanding of money and inflation.

REFERENCES

Irving Fisher analyzes the relation between prices and interest rates in Chapter 19 of *The Theory of Interest* (originally published in 1930; reprinted New York: Kelley, 1965). Self-generating inflation is treated by Phillip Cagan in his important article "The Monetary Dynamics of Hyperinflation"—which appears in *Studies in the Quantity Theory of Money*, edited by Milton Friedman (Chicago, Illinois: Chicago Univ. Press, 1956). The article by Dennis S. Karnosky, "Real Money Balances: A Misleading Indicator of Monetary Actions," which appears in the *Review* of the Federal Reserve Bank of St. Louis for February, 1974, pertains to what we have called the real cash balance mirage.

Terms to Remember

Real interest rate, expected and realized
Nominal interest rate
Gibson's paradox
Self-generating inflation
Passive accommodation doctrine
Real bills doctrine
Real cash balances mirage

[†] As if on this advice, the Fed did actually increase the monetary base by almost 8% during 1974. The base is a quantity under the relatively direct control of the Fed and ordinarily proportional to the total money stock. Actual growth of M was much lower during the second half of the year, but this was apparently due to an unforeseeable shift in the public's desired ratio of currency to demand deposits, rather than to deliberate policy.

INFLATIONARY FINANCE

THE GOVERNMENT REVENUE FROM MONEY CREATION

A government that can create money has at its disposal an easy means of financing its expenditures: For every dollar the government prints, it has that many extra dollars it can spend on military adventures, presidential palaces, wheat export subsidies, or any of the multitude of other amenities the government provides.

This source of revenue may prove more appealing to a country's rulers than ordinary taxes. Regular taxes often must be wheedled out of parliaments or congresses. Once the tax is officially authorized, it still must be physically snatched from someone's hand. This calls people's attention to the drain on the country's resources that the increased government spending entails, and leads the public to question whether the expenditures are really justified.

Monetary expansion is much easier. Legislative approval is often not required. The money just rolls off the presses, or appears as profits from the esoteric operations of the central bank. No IRS meanies are necessary.

The state lavishes services on the public. As far as anyone can tell, it has created these resources by white magic. We will investigate the true source of these resources in Chapter 7. In this chapter, we are mainly concerned with the quantity of resources the government can raise in this manner, and the inflationary implications thereof.

If the government creates all the money by itself (that is, if the banks are government owned or operate on one hundred percent reserves), whenever the nominal money supply increases by ΔM, it has $G = \Delta M$ extra dollars it can spend. Creating money on a large scale is liable to be inflationary, so we want to think in terms of the *real* resources $G/P = \Delta M/P$ that the government raises. As with m, t, and y, we will use a lowercase letter to represent this real quantity: $g = G/P$. In this chapter, the trick is to break g down into the product of two terms as follows:

$$g = \frac{\Delta M}{P}$$

$$= \frac{\Delta M}{M} \cdot \frac{M}{P} \tag{5-1}$$

$$\boxed{g = \frac{\Delta M}{M} \cdot \dot{m}} \tag{5-2}$$

The first term $(\Delta M/M)$ is the rate of growth of the nominal money supply, which is positively related to the inflation rate through the difference form of the quantity equation. The second term (m) is the quantity of real cash balances, which in equilibrium *decreases* with the rate of anticipated inflation. Thus the higher the expected rate of inflation, the greater will have to be the rate of monetary growth (and therefore actual inflation) necessary to raise a given quantity of resources.

AN EXAMPLE

To illustrate, suppose that in a certain Latin American country (call it Bolumbia), the real interest rate (r) is 5% per annum and the annual rate of growth of real income is 10%. Assume for the sake of simplicity that these values are relatively constant, regardless of Bolumbian monetary policy. The quantity of *real* cash balances desired at the current level of real income and various levels of the *nominal* interest rate is given in 1967 pesos in Table 5-1.

TABLE 5-1.   Demand for Money in Bolumbia

Nominal interest rate i (%)	Real cash balances $m = M/P$ (in millions of 1967 pesos)
5	200
10	180
15	160
20	140
25	120
30	100
35	80
40	60
45	40
50	20

What rate of monetary expansion and inflation would be required for the Bolumbian government to raise, say, 60 million 1967 pesos per year? That depends on the expected inflation rate. If initially people expect no inflation, then the nominal interest rate i would equal the real interest rate, which we have assumed to be 5%. According to Table 5-1, that means that m will be $200 million (1967). [†]Rearranging formula (5-2), we have

[†]The "dollar" sign was originally a peso sign. The original form was a superimposition of an uppercase P and a lowercase s. This evolved into the symbol $, which is still used in many Latin American countries. Its use to represent the U.S. dollar dates from the early days of this country, when most of the coins in circulation were Spanish. The version with two vertical strokes is a later imitation of the peso sign. It is based on the letters U and S, and specifically signifies the United States dollar.

$$\frac{\Delta M}{M} = \frac{g}{m}$$

$$= \frac{\$60 \text{ million } (1967)}{\$200 \text{ million } (1967)}$$

$$= 0.30 \qquad\qquad (5\text{-}3)$$

or 30%, so the money supply would have to increase at an annual rate of thirty percent. Assuming for the time being that velocity is constant, the difference form of the quantity equation[†] implies

$$\frac{\Delta P}{P} = (30\%) + (0\%) - (10\%)$$

$$= 20\%$$

so prices would rise by 20% each year.

This might work for a while, but eventually the Bolumbians would notice the inflation. After they have come to anticipate 20% inflation, the nominal interest rate will rise to 5% + 20% = 25%, and m will fall off to $120 million (1967). Thirty-percent monetary expansion would then yield only $36 million (1967) worth of resources each year. In order to get g back up to $60 million (1967), Eq. (5-3) implies that the Bolumbian government would have to increase the rate of monetary expansion to

$$\frac{\Delta M}{M} = \frac{\$60 \text{ million } (1967)}{\$120 \text{ million } (1967)}$$

$$= 0.50$$

or 50% per year. After velocity stabilizes at a new level, this implies

$$\frac{\Delta P}{P} = (50\%) + (0\%) - (10\%)$$

$$= 40\%$$

The necessary monetary expansion becomes very large when people catch on to the 40% inflation rate. Then $i = 40\% + 5\% = 45\%$, and m falls off to $40 million (1967). Fifty-percent monetary expansion would yield

---

[†] The student should have memorized Eqs. (3-11) and (3-12) by now.

only half this value, or $20 million (1967), each year. The target level of *g* would require

$$\frac{\Delta M}{M} = \frac{\$60 \text{ million } (1967)}{\$40 \text{ million } (1967)}$$

$$= 1.50$$

or 150% per year! With constant velocity and our assumed 10% real growth rate, this implies 140% inflation each year!

At this point we have run off the end of our table, so we cannot say what actual inflation rate would be necessary to raise 60 million 1967 pesos worth of real resources when people have come to expect 150% inflation. In a more realistic table of real cash balances as a function of the nominal interest rate, *m* would keep getting smaller and smaller as *i* increased, but would never quite reach zero. In that case, we could go on raising 60 million pesos forever, with astronomical inflation rates.

In this example we have considered stationary states in which velocity is constant. However, velocity is higher (*m* lower) in each successive state, so there must be an intervening period when velocity is rising, and therefore inflation even higher than we have indicated. Handling this effect precisely involves more complicated mathematics than we have been using. It suffices to note that the increase in velocity will augment the inflation, rather than diminish it.

FULLY ANTICIPATED INFLATION

In the above example, there was always more inflation than people anticipated. When they expected none, they got 20%. When they expected 20%, they got 40%. When they were ready for 40%, they got a whopping 140%. What would happen with a constant inflation rate that people had come to anticipate correctly?

A 10% fully anticipated inflation rate, for instance, would imply $i = 10\% + 5\% = 15\%$, so *m* would be $160 million (1967). In a steady state with constant velocity, the monetary expansion rate would have to be 10% + 10% − 0% = 20%. The value of *g* would then be 20% of 160, or $32 million (1967) per year. In this manner, we can figure out the value of g for each nominal interest rate, as shown in Table 5-2.

TABLE 5-2

i (%)	$\left(\frac{\Delta P}{P}\right)^*$ (%)	$\frac{\Delta P}{P}$ (%)	$\frac{\Delta M}{M}$ (%)	m (millions of 1967 pesos)	g (millions of 1967 pesos)
5	0	0	10	200	20
10	5	5	15	180	27
15	10	10	20	160	32
20	15	15	25	140	35
25	20	20	30	120	36
30	25	25	35	100	35
35	30	30	40	80	32
40	35	35	45	60	27
45	40	40	50	40	20
50	45	45	55	20	11

The figures in this table illustrate an important phenomenon. As the monetary expansion rate (and therefore the inflation rate and nominal interest rate) increases with fully anticipated inflation, g rises for a while. But eventually it reaches a maximum, 36 million 1967 Bolumbian pesos at an inflation rate of 20% in this example. Thereafter m falls off faster than $\Delta M/M$ rises, so that g actually decreases.

It bears emphasis that 36 million pesos is *not* the most that can be raised by inflationary finance. We demonstrated in the previous section, using exactly the same data, that it is perfectly possible to raise 60 million pesos every year, but only at the cost of a runaway inflation in which people are continually surprised by how high actual inflation is. The 36 million pesos figure is merely the most that can be raised with *fully antici-pated* inflation.

[*Note*: These two problems require the student to draw together his understanding of the quantity equation, real versus nominal interest rates, and inflationary finance. They are a good test of the student's grasp of a large part of the material of this book.]

Problem 5-1

What is the revenue maximizing fully anticipated inflation rate in Bolumbia if instead the real interest rate is 10% and real income grows by 5% each year? What are the corresponding monetary expansion and inflation rates? Continue to use the demand for real cash balances schedule of Table 5-1.

Problem 5-2

(a) Using the data of Problem 5-1, but no longer assuming fully anticipated inflation, what rate of monetary expansion and inflation will be necessary to raise $36 million (1967) each year if people expect no inflation?

(b) If people expect the inflation rate of part (a)?

(c) If people expect the inflation rate of part (b)?

(d) If people expect the inflation rate of part (c)?

Assume velocity is constant in each case.

RUNAWAY INFLATION

One important implication of the maximum revenue obtainable from fully anticipated inflation is that any level of *g* less than this value can be obtained with a constant inflation rate, while any level of *g* above this value requires runaway inflation that increases without bound. As long as the target is kept below this critical level, there will be no tendency for the inflation to get out of control as long as the economy does not have the conditions necessary for self-generating inflation.

Does "monetary irresponsibility" (i.e., printing money to meet government expenses) lead inevitably to runaway inflation? Definitely not. Substantial resources can usually be raised without any inflation at all (20 million 1967 pesos with a 10% monetary growth rate in Table 5-2). A higher level of monetary irresponsibility leads to inflation, but only a constant rate of inflation as long as irresponsibility is practiced with moderation. Only *excessive irresponsibility* leads to runaway inflation.

The revenue-maximizing fully anticipated inflation rate depends critically on the shape of the demand for money schedule. If at every interest rate people desired ten times as many real cash balances, the government could raise $36 \times 10 = \$360$ million (1967) per year with a constant 20% inflation rate. Furthermore, if the demand for m didn't fall off so quickly, the revenue maximizing inflation rate would be much higher.

In a study of European hyperinflations after World War I and World War II, Robert Barro estimated that the government of a typical country could divert about 15% of national income to itself with a fully anticipated inflation rate of 140% *per month*! Such an inflation rate, if compounded daily, would imply that 20 million dollars at the end of the year would be worth as little as one dollar at the beginning of the year! Our table, which was designed with arithmetic simplicity in mind rather than realism, greatly understates the actual revenue-maximizing rate.

Not satisfied with the large sum that can be raised by rapid but steady inflation, some of the European governments involved in the inflations studied by Barro tried to raise even more, and truly runaway inflation set in. During the post-World War I German inflation, the inflation rate hit a peak of 32,400% per month. One German mark in August, 1922 had the same purchasing power as 10.2 billion (10,200,000,000) marks in November, 1923. But this was nothing compared with Hungary after World War II. From August of 1945 to July of 1946, the number of Hungarian pengös in circulation increased by a factor of 11.9 septillion (11,900,000,000,000,000,000,000,000). Over the same period, the purchasing power of the pengö fell by a factor of 3.81 *octillion* (3,810,000,000,000,000,000,000,000,000).† The fact that the price level increased more than in proportion to the nominal money supply does not mean that the solution to the country's inflation problem was to "print more money." Rather, it indicates the decline in desired real cash balances brought about by the inflationary monetary expansion.

---

† These figures are from Cagan's related study of hyperinflations, cited at the end of Chapter 4.

FRACTIONAL RESERVE BANKING

One of the first assumptions of this chapter was that the government creates all of the money in circulation. In most economies, however, the money supply consists both of hand-to-hand currency and fractionally backed bank deposits. The government only creates "high-powered money," a name for currency plus bank reserves.

Let us suppose that the total money supply is some multiple k times high-powered money. This k is known as the bank expansion multiplier, and depends on the reserves the banks keep and the public's preferences for currency as opposed to checking accounts. In the United States, it is currently equal to about 2.5. If the money supply increases by ΔM, only $\Delta M/k$ of the increase corresponds to new high-powered money the government has issued. The difference $\Delta M - \Delta M/k$ is the net money creation of the banks.

The U.S. Treasury does not simply regard new high-powered money as current revenue. However, when the Federal Reserve System permanently increases the quantity of high-powered money, it usually lends money indirectly to the Treasury by increasing its holdings of U.S. Treasury bills, notes, or bonds. The Treasury pays the Fed interest on these securities, but the Fed turns around and returns its profits, composed mostly of these interest payments, to the Treasury. Therefore, the Treasury in effect is receiving a permanent, interest-free loan of the amount of the increase in high-powered money. It may as well have received a bequest from an eccentric billionaire as far as its command over resources goes.

Like the Treasury, a private bank would never enter new money creation on its profit and loss statement as current income. But it does enter income from earning assets. A monetary expansion that permanently increases the money supply by ΔM will permanently increase the earning assets of the banking system by $\Delta M - \Delta M/k$. If the interest rate is i, the annual income of the banking system will go up by $i(\Delta M - \Delta M/k)$ assuming the banks are not permitted to compete with one another for deposits by paying interest on checking accounts and ignoring their operating expenses. The reader may recollect that the present value of a perpetual stream of annual payments of size A is A/i. Therefore, the present value of the banks' income is increased by $i(\Delta M - \Delta M/k)/i = \Delta M/k$, which is just equal to the banks' share of the new money creation, provided the i at which the banks' shareholders discount future earnings equals the i at which the banks make loans.

In practice, the banks will have to lower the rate at which they lend in order to attract borrowers. To this extent, the owners of the banks will not receive all of the new purchasing power, but will have to share it with the banks' loan customers. In competing for new loans, the banks may so depress their lending rate that they will actually be worse off, and their customers will benefit by more than $\Delta M - \Delta M/k$.

A further complication is that the government is likely to be one of the banks' largest loan customers, since the banking system's earning assets include many government bonds. It is therefore very difficult to sort out the ultimate beneficiaries of the monetary expansion when there is fractional reserve banking. All we can say is that the revenues from inflationary finance are shared by the government, the owners of the private banks, and the nongovernmental borrowers from the banking system, such as corporations and homebuyers.

It could be argued that political pressure to have the banking system lower the interest rate (see Chapter 4) amounts to a form of inflationary finance. The industries that benefit from the lowered interest rates could instead be given grants from the Treasury that were raised by inflationary finance with a 100% reserve banking system. Granting them low-interest loans through the fractional reserve banking system amounts to roughly the same thing. It merely substitutes the private banking middleman for the governmental middleman.

DEBASING THE CURRENCY

It is often contended that the value of the monetary unit is determined by its metallic content or backing.[†] This is fallacious, but contains a half-truth.

[†] See, for example, "Counterfeiting in Roman Britain," by George C. Boon in *Scientific American* (December, 1974), pp. 120–130.

Imagine the following scenario: A certain country starts on a simple gold (or silver) coin standard with free coinage, so that the value of the monetary unit equals the value of its metallic content. Gradually, paper certificates are substituted for the gold coins on a one-for-one basis. At first, the paper certificates are freely convertible into gold coins. People tend to prefer the paper money because it is easier to handle.[†] Eventually, the right to redeem the paper notes in gold is removed and the owners of the few remaining coins in circulation are required to turn them in for paper. At first, 100% gold backing is kept for the inconvertible notes, but finally the government sells the gold backing on the international bullion market. The country's currency is then pure fiat money.

There is no reason why removing the gold backing in this manner would be inflationary per se, as long as the number of paper notes remains constant (or is allowed to grow only at the rate the gold coin money supply would have grown). The government is able to use the proceeds of the gold sale to finance current operations or retire debt without levying taxes, but this is not inflationary; society is actually wealthier to the extent that it is now able to make nonmonetary use of the gold that formerly was tied up as currency or backing for the currency. The purchasing power of the notes the day they are made inconvertible derives from the purchasing power they had the day before, as modified by any change in their supply relative to the country's demand for money. Their ability to be converted is irrelevant, since virtually no one wanted to convert them anyway. Similarly, their value will undergo no particular change the day the backing is sold off.

However, once the backing is removed, the road is open for inflationary finance, and few governments fail to take advantage of the opportunity. When 100% backing was required, every new note the government put into circulation corresponded to an equal value of gold the government had to lock up in its vaults, so there was no fiscal advantage to creating new notes. But if it can issue unbacked or partially backed notes, it creates more purchasing power than it is required to put away. The temptation is almost irresistible.

[†] According to Alexander Solzhenitsyn, bank customers in prerevolutionary Russia would often bribe clerks to pay out notes instead of gold (*August 1914*, New York: Bantam, 1974, p. 75).

Often the actual gold or silver content of the coins in circulation is gradually reduced. This is referred to as "debasing" the coinage. Suppose the currency originally consists of gold "crowns" each containing 1.00 gram of gold. The monarch soon discovers that he can mint 9 crowns worth of gold into 10 new crowns, each of which contains 0.90 gram of gold alloyed with less expensive metals to make a full-sized coin. The profit he makes doing this is called "seigniorage." At first this process is not inflationary, provided the relative price of gold versus goods is determined in international markets and is independent of developments in this one small country. In that case, roughly one old crown containing 1.00 gram of gold will be melted down by private citizens into bullion† to be sold abroad, for every new crown containing 0.90 grams of gold that the king puts into circulation. The money supply and the price level will remain approximately constant. To see this, suppose first that an equal number of old crowns were not melted down as the new crowns were introduced. The money stock would increase and the domestic price level would rise. A gram of gold could be obtained by melting one of the old coins, which still comprise the bulk of the money supply. It would be profitable to do so, because the gold could buy more abroad as bullion than it could at home as a one-crown coin. On the other hand, it wouldn't pay to melt down more than an equal number of the old crowns right away, because that would decrease the money supply and therefore the domestic price level; the one-crown coins, even the debased ones, would actually be worth more than 1.00 grams of gold, so melting would be unprofitable and quickly come to an end.

However, the situation changes once all the old crowns have disappeared from circulation. (This tendency for "bad money to drive out good" is known as Gresham's law.) When the last one has disappeared, the monarch can still obtain 10 crowns worth of goods for 9 crowns worth of gold, so he goes on minting the 0.90 gram coins. The money supply increases and the price level (including the price of gold) increases. Soon he has to pay 9.5 inflated crowns for the 0.90 grams of gold he puts into 10 one-crown coins, but this still pays. Finally, it costs 10 crowns to mint 10 crowns. The purchasing power of the crown is again proportional to its

† Bullion is uncoined gold or silver in bar form.

gold content. What does the monarch do for revenue now? Probably he will change the gold content to 0.80 grams and repeat the whole process. Each debasement will be associated with continued deterioration of the value of the crown. Its purchasing power will decline roughly in proportion to the amount of gold it contains. This is the sense in which it is half true that the currency's metallic content determines its purchasing power.

Yet it is not the debasement that causes the inflation, but rather the increase in the quantity of crowns outstanding. This increase is made possible by the debasement, and may be politically "inevitable," but economically speaking it is not a necessary consequence. In theory, the monarch could refrain from minting more debased crowns than there were original crowns. When he got the gold content down to zero, the country would essentially have the fiat money we described at the beginning of this section. But it is unlikely that he would quit at this point. The resources he can obtain while exercising this restraint are equal in value to the nation's original money supply. It is a once-and-for-all profit obtainable by replacing the gold money with paper money or token coins. In addition to this profit, there is also the annual income to be had through classic inflationary finance. The latter may net as much *each year* as the once-and-for-all gain from the former. In terms of the Bolumbian economy discussed above (Table 5-2), replacing gold coins with fiat money would release $200 million (1967) worth of gold. This revenue would not be repeatable. Expanding the money supply could then bring in an additional $36 million (1967) each year, forever, even without runaway inflation. With a more realistic demand for money schedule, the latter revenue might be more like 36 million *per month*. It is important not to confuse these two sources of revenue made possible by removing the currency's metallic backing. The truth in the statement that the currency's metallic content determines its value rests with the assumption that the government will not be able to resist the second source of revenue. Historically, this is a fairly safe assumption.

HARD MONEY

In a sense, metallic currency is socially wasteful. It could be replaced with a stable paper currency and society would be wealthier in real terms because it would be able to make industrial or artistic use of the metal that would otherwise be tied up as money. As long as the government issues the same number of paper dollars as there would have been dollars with full metallic backing, the purchasing power of your money will be secure. Surely gold and silver coins and backing are evidence of irrationality on the part of those who insist on them.

A similar argument could be made for bicycle locks and chains.[†] If metal locks could be replaced with symbolic paper locks, resources would be released that could be used productively elsewhere. As long as thieves honor paper locks as they would metal locks, your bike will be perfectly secure. Surely hardened steel and phosphor bronze shackles are evidence of irrationality on the part of those who insist on them.

Pure economics is unable to tell us whether the politician is more to be trusted than the common bike thief. Perhaps, as Keynes contended, gold is merely a "barbarous relic." Or perhaps we should follow the advice of the radical pamphleteer William Cobbett who urged people to cash bank notes for specie as quickly as possible, as in the following message "addressed especially to women":

> Stayed dames, put it by with those silks and lace, that you have so long preserved as memorials of your early conquests! Lovely maidens, hug it to those bosoms, which would almost warm the metal into flesh and blood!—Faith, I must stop, or I shall be myself on fire.[‡]

Extreme insistence on a metallic standard in spite of the resources it ties up and in spite of the uncontrollability of the rate of monetary growth is not so ludicrous when we take into account the threat of covert taxation through inflationary finance. A metallic monetary system would not provide complete protection against this tax, because the state could still seize the backing for more convenient gold or silver certificates, and could try to prohibit the use of full-bodied coins in order to create as much demand as possible for its fiat money. Nevertheless, the possibility of black market

---

[†] This analogy is due to Joel Holmes.

[‡] (1821) Quoted in F.W. Fetter, *Development of British Monetary Orthodoxy, 1797–1875* (Cambridge, Massachusetts: Harvard Univ. Press, 1965, p. 108).

circulation of these coins would imply some limitation of the potential for inflationary finance.

Perhaps the resurrection of a metallic standard is wishful thinking. But as long as we are wishing, which metal should we wish for? The two with an historical role as money are gold and silver. At the beginning of the eighteenth century, silver was the world's money.[†] Through the eighteenth and nineteenth centuries, gold gradually displaced silver, mainly because of a series of bungled governmental efforts to supplement silver with gold on a bimetallic basis. By 1910 gold was so entrenched that it would have been ridiculous to suggest switching back to silver. However, gold never fully recovered from the complications of global inflationary finance during World War I. From 1933 until 1975, Americans were not allowed even to own gold except in nonmonetary forms. Since 1971 there has been no de facto link between the dollar and gold. Today, gold is just as dead as money as is silver. Perhaps gold is farther gone than silver, since the present generation in America at least remembers when coins with a significant silver content circulated from hand to hand, while it is harder to find anyone who remembers the circulation of gold coins. Technically, silver quarters and dimes were originally just expensive token coins whose monetary significance was that they were exchangeable for gold-backed dollars, rather than that they contained silver. Nevertheless, the value of the silver they contained was comparable to their purchasing power. This means that a large portion of the population would be able to form a notion by heft alone of what the purchasing power of say a ten gram silver coin would be.

Given that silver is at least even with gold today, which would make the better money? A desirable monetary metal should have a prospect of a relatively stable rate of production. It would be ideal if this rate of production corresponded to price stability, but any constant rate of production would be far superior to an erratic rate of production that produced inflation one year and deflation the next. Over 70% of the world's gold is produced by one country, the Union of South Africa, and this gold comes from a few mines located within a small district including the Transvaal

[†] See John Law, *Money and Trade Considered* (originally published in 1705; reprinted, New York: Kelley, 1966), Chapter 1.

and the Witwatersrand. It is hard to predict whether the white government in South Africa will remain in power over the next several decades or if the government—and control of the mines—will change hands abruptly. The marketing strategy of a secure monopolist is to hold back production so as to keep prices up. But the marketing strategy of an insecure monopolist who fears he may be expropriated is likely to be to get as much output out as fast as he can before he loses control of the mines. When he sells this output he will be in competition with the new owners, so more will appear on the market than under simple monopoly. We therefore must conclude that the outlook for the stability of the rate of gold production is not very good.

A comparable fraction of the world's silver, on the other hand, is produced by five countries: Mexico, the United States, Peru, Canada, and the Soviet Union. †None of these has a clear lead, so the international market for silver is relatively competitive and hence not very sensitive to changes in the politics of any one country. It is hard to conceive of any more than two of these countries agreeing on anything, let alone trusting one another to hold back production as a cartel. Furthermore, within each of these countries the silver is distributed among a large number of widely scattered mines, so that the world silver supply is fairly immune to changes in borders or in the productivity of individual deposits.

On the basis of stability of supply, therefore, silver would seem to be a better choice (assuming we had a choice) of a metallic money. Unfortunately the hard-money literature still has a somewhat out-of-date obsession with gold.

†Data from *The World Almanac*, 1974 edition, p. 90 (New York: Doubleday, 1974), and *The Oxford Economic Atlas of the World*, 4th edition, p. 49 (London: Oxford Univ. Press, 1972).

REFERENCES

See Martin Bailey, "The Welfare Cost of Inflationary Finance," *Journal of Political Economy* (April, 1956), and Cagan's article on hyperinflations, cited at the end of Chapter 4. An interesting article on what constitutes a "true" metallic standard is Milton Friedman's "Real and Pseudo Gold Standards," *Journal of Law and Economics* (October, 1961).

Terms to Remember

Inflationary finance
Fully anticipated inflation
Runaway inflation
Fractional reserve banking
Debasement[†]
Seigniorage
Gresham's law

[†] This is *not* part of a house.

THE INFLATION—
UNEMPLOYMENT TRADEOFF

THE PHILLIPS CURVE

In the 1950s an English economist named Phillips noticed that over a long period of time the United Kingdom experienced a stable negative relationship between inflation and unemployment.[†] As shown in Fig. 6-1, the United States had a similar experience in the years 1959-67. A line drawn through these points is called a *Phillips curve*. It was originally believed that the existence of the Phillips curve gave the economy an unfortunate long-run tradeoff between inflation and unemployment: Low unemployment could be had only at the expense of high inflation, while low inflation would necessitate high unemployment.

[†] A.W. Phillips, "The Relation between Unemployment and the Rate of Change of Money Wage Rates in the United Kingdom, 1861-1957," *Economica* (November, 1958).

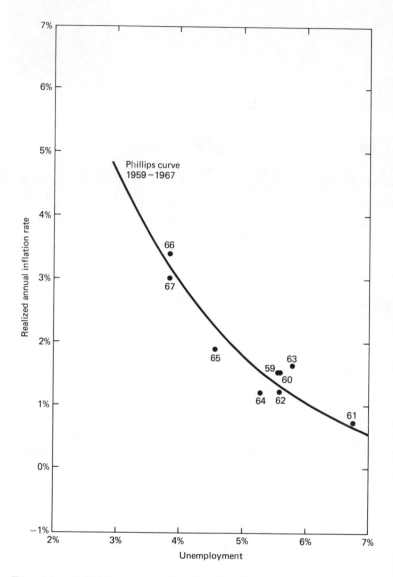

Fig. 6-1. A Phillips curve for the United States, 1959-67. Source: *Economic Report of the President,* **1974.**

In Fig. 6-2, we have added points for the periods 1952-55 and 1969-72. These points clearly do not lie on our original Phillips curve. Nevertheless, they do seem to trace out Phillips curves of their own. Thus, while there does seem to be a Phillips-type tradeoff in the short run, the location of the Phillips curve apparently *shifts* over time. There is no eternal Phillips relation.

THE NATURAL UNEMPLOYMENT RATE HYPOTHESIS

Why should the Phillips curve shift over time? Indeed, why should there be a short-run Phillips tradeoff in the first place? Let us take the second question first. To answer it, we must ask, "Why do people without jobs remain unemployed?"[†] There are countless reasons, most of them unrelated to inflation. Some people live in areas associated with particular industries that are dying out. Some people face job discrimination because of their skin color or sex or because they speak the wrong language. Some like to collect unemployment benefits and aren't really trying very hard to get a job.[‡] Some don't have enough job experience to make it worth an employer's while to pay them the legal minimum wage. Some don't have a friend or relative at the union hiring hall. Some have been offered jobs, but only at an unsatisfactory rate of pay.

Hold it! We may be able to do something with that last reason. How much pay is "satisfactory"? That depends partly on a person's qualifications, *and partly on the cost of living*. If a jobseeker expects prices to be high, he (or she) will regard only a *high* wage as satisfactory. Conversely, if she (or he) expects prices to be low, she will be more likely to regard a *low* wage as satisfactory.

If there is inflationary pressure in the economy, employers whose products are enjoying brisk demand will be able to make higher-paying job offers than they would have otherwise. If the inflation is unanticipated, jobseekers will think that the higher job offers represent an increased

---

[†] Leo Rosten tells a story about a man who was asked, "Why do you always answer every question with another question?" The answer? "Why not?"

[‡] See Martin Feldstein, "The Economics of the New Unemployment," *The Public Interest* (Fall, 1973).

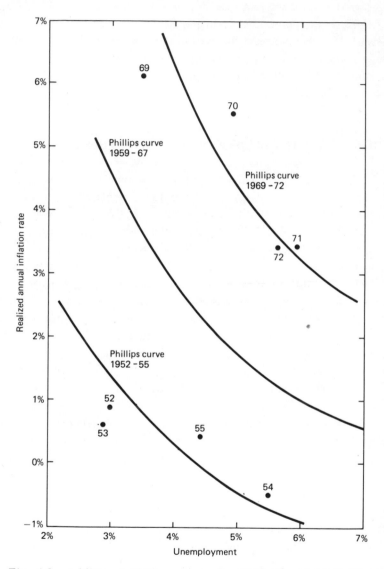

Fig. 6-2. Additional Phillips curves for 1952–55 and 1969–72. The curve for 1959–67 is the one from Fig. 6-1 (same source).

demand for their particular services and will not recognize that they merely reflect a general excess demand that is driving up everyone's wages, and the prices of all goods, including the goods they buy. This means that when prices are rising unexpectedly, jobseekers will overestimate the purchasing power of any given wage offer. Some of those who would otherwise have continued searching and therefore have remained unemployed for a while until a more appropriate job came along will instead accept jobs with wage rates that will later prove to be "unsatisfactorily" low in real terms. In this manner, *unexpected inflation will reduce unemployment*.

On the other hand, if prices are *falling* unexpectedly, jobseekers will *underestimate* the purchasing power of any given wage offer. They may be offered jobs at wages that will later prove to be satisfactory, but they will go on searching in vain for a job with a higher nominal wage in order to get the real wage they feel they should be able to command. Therefore *unexpected deflation will increase unemployment*. In either case, what matters is not the actual inflation rate, but rather the *difference* between actual and expected inflation.

If inflation or deflation is fully anticipated, jobseekers will judge the real value of a given job offer correctly. There should be no more or less unemployment than if prices were always stable. This unemployment rate towards which the economy tends when inflation is fully anticipated is called the "natural unemployment rate."

For any given level of the expected inflation rate $(\Delta P/P)^*$, there will be a downward-sloping *short-run Phillips curve (SPRC)* showing a tradeoff between the *actual* inflation rate and the level of unemployment, that is valid only in the short run. In Fig. 6-3, $SRPC_0$ corresponds to $(\Delta P/P)^* = 0$. If $\Delta P/P$ is actually zero, unemployment will equal the natural unemployment rate U_n $SRPC_b$ corresponds to $(\Delta P/P)^* = b$. If $\Delta P/P$ actually equals b, U will again be U_n. If actual $\Delta P/P$ is greater than b, U will be less than U_n. If $\Delta P/P$ is less than b, U will be greater than U_n. Similarly, $SRPC_a$ and $SRPC_c$ correspond to inflation rate a and deflation rate c. Just as in the case of interest rates, if a given inflation rate continues long enough, people will come to expect it to continue. In the long run, for any given constant rate of inflation, expected inflation will eventually catch up with actual inflation and unemployment will return to U_n. The *long-run Phillips curve (LRPC)* is therefore vertical at U_n.

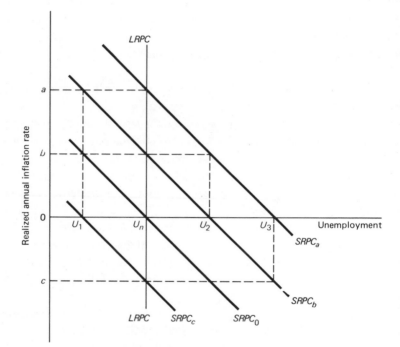

Fig. 6-3. The long-run Phillips curve (*LRPC*) and the corresponding family of short-run Phillips curves (*SRPC_a*, etc.) for different levels of expected inflation.

UNEMPLOYMENT-ORIENTED INFLATION POLICY

If people expect no inflation, the government could reduce U to U_1 in Fig. 6-3 by engineering an inflation rate equal to b. However, it could not do this forever, since people would come to expect this inflation, causing the Phillips curve to shift from $SRPC_0$ to $SRPC_b$. At $\Delta P/P = b$, U would return to the natural rate U_n. To keep U at U_1, the government would have to raise $\Delta P/P$ to a, and then even higher as expectations caught up with this rate. It is therefore impossible to use the Phillips curve relation to lower unemployment below U_n permanently without ever-accelerating inflation. This law has become known as the "acceleration principle." In order to lower unemployment permanently with inflation, it is not sufficient merely to raise the inflation rate by a constant amount each year, say from 3 to 4 to 5 to 6%. If people saw this pattern of inflation rates, they would start to form more sophisticated projections of the inflation rate and would predict 7% for the following year instead of simply assuming 6% would continue. Seven-percent inflation in that year would therefore just yield the natural unemployment rate, so 8% inflation would become necessary to lower U below U_n. In the end, runaway inflation will have to set in for this policy, just as it does with the low-interest rate policy, the real cash balance mirage, and excessive inflationary finance. One of the elder statesmen of monetary theory has expressed the acceleration principle rather nicely. Observing that we have reached the stage where merely "to slow down inflation produces a recession," he goes on to say

> We now have a tiger by the tail. . . . If the tiger (of inflation) is freed he will eat us up; yet if he runs faster and faster while we desperately hold on, we are *still* finished! I'm glad I won't be here to see the final outcome . . . .[†]

On the other hand, if $(\Delta P/P)^*$ has grown to a and the authorities

---

[†] F.A. Hayek, 1969 speech reprinted in his book *A Tiger by the Tail*, edited by Sudha Shenoy (London: The Institute of Economic Affairs, 1972), p. 112.

suddenly slam on the monetary brakes to bring P to a screeching halt, U will jump to U_3 along $SRPC_a$. Rather than throw the economy through the windshield with a drastic counterinflationary campaign, a government that was determined to end inflation might be well advised to do so gradually.[†] If inflation were first reduced to b, U would only rise to U_2. As $(\Delta P/P)^*$ fell to b, U would fall back to U_n. Then $\Delta P/P$ could safely be lowered to zero, with U rising temporarily to U_2 along $SRPC_b$, and finally falling back to U_n as people came to expect price stability.

Problem 6-1

In Catalonia, the short-run Phillips curves have the equation

$$\frac{\Delta P}{P} = 8 - 2U + \left(\frac{\Delta P}{P}\right)^*$$

where U and the inflation rates are in percent.

(a) What is the natural unemployment rate U_n?

(b) How much inflation would be necessary to lower U to 2% if people expect no inflation?

(c) If people expect the inflation rate of part (b)?

IS THE NATURAL RATE OPTIMAL?

The natural rate has the desirable property that no one is bamboozled into accepting a job whose real compensation is insufficient in retrospect, nor into *refusing* a job whose real compensation will prove *sufficient* in retrospect. It therefore has a lot to be said for it.

Nevertheless, there are many factors other than judicious search contributing to the unemployment rate. These other factors may make the "natural" rate higher (or lower) than would be desirable in a perfect

---

[†] Of course, we dismiss the possibility of a government with sufficient credibility that it can announce it is going to end inflation and people will believe it.

society. If possible, these other factors should be attacked directly. But barring that, many economists argue that it is desirable to reduce U a little at the expense of some unanticipated inflation, at least for a while. They argue that the inflation and its costs are off in the future, while the gain in employment is immediate. Still it should be remembered that the reduction in employment comes about largely through the mismatching of workers to jobs, so that the economic benefits of the rise in employment are open to doubt. There is also a technical problem for the political scientists to work out: How is it possible for a democratic government deliberately to pursue a policy of fooling the people? How can the public's right hand not know what its left hand is up to?

MONEY AND BUSINESS FLUCTUATIONS

There is a well-known historical relation between money and business activity. Booms are associated with monetary expansions, while depressions are associated with monetary contractions.

The short-run Phillips curve relation, taken together with the quantity theory, gives us one possible explanation of this correlation: As the rate of monetary expansion grows, the inflation rate grows. This inflation is largely unanticipated, so unemployment falls and measured output rises. When the monetary expansion comes to an end or is reversed, deflation sets in (or at least inflation doesn't proceed as fast as expected). The Phillips curve gives temporarily high levels of unemployment, which result in low values of income.

Another possible explanation (which may amount to the same thing) is based on Walras' law, which we introduced in Chapter 2: A monetary expansion causes prices to rise, but only with a lag. In the meantime there is an excess supply of money, which implies a net excess demand for goods in general.[†] This net excess demand will appear to merchants and workers

---

[†] There would not necessarily be an excess demand for *all* goods, but only a *net* excess demand. There may be an excess demand for some goods and an excess supply of others. All Walras' law implies is that the total of the excess demands must exceed the total of the excess supplies by the amount of the excess supply of money.

as an unusual briskness of business—a boom. On the other hand, a monetary contraction will lead to a temporary excess demand for money and a net excess supply of ordinary goods until the price level can fall to its new equilibrium. Business will be slow and a recession or depression will appear.

Unfortunately, it is extremely hard to tell whether it is really the fluctuations in the money supply that are causing the fluctuations in the level of output, or vice versa. The extraordinary contraction of the U.S. money supply from 1930 to 1933 is often credited with the Great Depression of the 1930s.[†] However, a case could be made that it was the depression that caused the monetary contraction instead. Banks held large quantities of farm mortgages. The year 1930 was a disastrous one for farmers, who were afflicted both by crop failures and the loss of export markets. This agricultural depression led to defaults on farmers' bank loans, which in turn jeopardized the liquidity of the banks. A wave of bank runs set in, bank credit collapsed, and the money supply, to the extent that it consisted of fractional reserve bank deposits, dwindled. Similar stories could be told for most of the other depressions in history: Bad business causes bank failures, which reduce the money supply.

Among those who regard monetary disturbances as the major cause of business fluctuations, there are two schools of thought. The "Chicago" school, headed by Milton Friedman, subscribes to a relatively straightforward version of the way money affects business. According to this view, a monetary expansion leads to a temporary excess of money balances. People own more money than they want to keep on average, so they get rid of it, by spending it on immediate consumption goods, on consumer durables such as automobiles, or on business investments. This increased spending shows up directly as higher income, both real and nominal. Eventually it just leads to higher prices but in the short run there are important real effects. The policy prescription of this school is a constant monetary growth rate.

The other "Austrian" school, headed by Nobel Prize laureate F.A.

[†] See Milton Friedman and Anna Jacobson Schwartz, *A Monetary History of the United States, 1867-1960* (NBER, 1963), especially Chapter 7 (published separately as *The Great Contraction*).

Hayek,[†] emphasizes the lowering of the real interest rate that is temporarily made possible by bank expansion. The firms that borrow the new money are led to initiate projects that do not reflect the true intertemporal consumption tastes of the consumers. When the bank expansion comes to an end, the real interest rate goes back up to its natural level, and these firms find that their projects are no longer profitable. They fail or cut back production, and the depression sets in. The policy prescription of this school is one hundred percent reserve banking, in order to prevent the original artificial credit expansion.

Whether or not we believe with these schools that money is the *principal* cause of the major business fluctuations of the past two centuries in industrialized countries, it is clear that money can have *some* disturbing effect on output and employment. Perhaps it has a right to be considered innocent until proven guilty beyond the shadow of a doubt. Yet it should definitely be high on our list whenever we "round up the usual suspects."

REFERENCES

On the Phillips curve, see Irving Fisher, "I Discovered the Phillips Curve," *Journal of Political Economy* (March/April, 1973; a reprint of a 1926 article originally entitled "A Statistical Relation between Unemployment and Price Changes"). The natural rate hypothesis was put forward by Milton Friedman in his American Economics Association presidential address, *American Economic Review*, March, 1968. Compare James Tobin's presidential address a couple of years later, in the *AER* for March, 1972. The notion of an optimal balance between unemployment reduction and price stability is developed by Edmund S. Phelps, *Inflation Policy and Unemployment Theory* (New York: Norton, 1972).

The best place to start for the Chicago approach to "Money and Business Cycles" is the article of that name by Milton Friedman, *Review of Economics and Statistics* (February, 1963, Supplement). (This article also appears in Friedman's book *The Optimum Quantity of Money,* Chicago, Illinois: Aldine, 1969.) James Tobin rebuts part of Friedman's argument in "Money and Income: Post Hoc Ergo Propter Hoc?," *Quarterly Journal of Economics* (May, 1970). For the "Austrian" approach, see Chapter 20 in Ludwig von Mises' *Human Action* (New Haven, Connecticut: Yale Univ. Press, 1963), Irving Fisher's *One Hundred Percent Money*

[†] See his column in *The New York Times*, November 15, 1974.

(New York: Adelphi, 1936), and Murray Rothbard's *America's Great Depression* (Princeton, New Jersey: Van Nostrand, 1963).

Terms to Remember

> Phillips curve
> Short-run Phillips curve
> Long-run Phillips curve
> Natural unemployment rate
> Natural rate hypothesis
> Acceleration principle
> Chicago School
> Austrian School

SIDE EFFECTS
OF INFLATION

THE INFLATIONARY REDISTRIBUTION OF INCOME:
DEBTOR–CREDITOR

Three different types of income redistribution may come about as a consequence of inflation. The redistribution that receives the most public attention is that between debtors and creditors. If I have lent you money and the price level goes up more than we expected, I will lose real purchasing power, and you will gain. My loss exactly equals your gain. If prices unexpectedly fall, I will gain and you will lose. This debtor–creditor redistribution only occurs to the extent that the price change is unanticipated. If we both correctly foresaw inflation, we would have simply agreed upon a higher interest rate, so that you would have had to pay me back that much more, in nominal terms, than if we had correctly foreseen constant prices.

This sort of redistribution poses a problem for the monetary authorities if they wish to terminate an inflation that has come to be anticipated. Today people expect considerable inflation to continue. Borrowers such as corporations and homebuyers are agreeing to pay unusually high nominal interest rates because they assume that the dollars they will have to repay will have become substantially cheaper to acquire (in terms of goods and labor) as the payments come due. If the monetary authorities switch to a less expansionary monetary policy and succeed in terminating inflation, the real burden of this indebtedness will rise, just as it did in the early 1930s when people expected relatively constant prices but instead encountered several years of deflation. The possibility of widespread bankruptcies and foreclosures is a very serious one.

It is too late to change the terms of contracts that have already been written, but one way to prevent this arbitrary and disruptive redistribution in the future is to contract loans in terms of purchasing power. Repayments would be agreed upon in terms of constant (say 1967) dollars. When the repayment is due, the agreed-upon sum in 1967 dollars would be multiplied by the latest price index to arrive at the number of current dollars actually to be paid. In constant dollars the interest rate would be much lower than we have become used to—perhaps 2 or 4% per annum, instead of 8 to 11%. Purchasing power loans would take much of the guesswork out of borrowing and lending.

Purchasing power loans (sometimes called "indexed" loans) should not be confused with "variable-rate" loans. A variable rate loan is a relatively long-term loan in which the interest payments are tied to whatever nominal interest rates on short-term loans happen to be as the payments fall due. These variable-rate loans do not take the guesswork out of borrowing and lending, because future short-term nominal interest rates will contain the market's latest guess about inflation for the immediate future. It is true that these loans substitute a more educated guess for a less educated guess: At the beginning of 1980, the market will have a better idea of what inflation will be during 1980 than it does now. But still, it will only be a guess. Furthermore, with variable-rate loans the borrower and lender have no way of knowing what sort of real rate they will end up paying or receiving.

To illustrate this distinction, suppose you lend me $1000.00 for 2 years, and we both agree that 2% is a satisfactory real interest rate. If we could be sure prices would remain constant, I would sign a contract agreeing to repay $20.00 next year and $1020.00 the following year, a total of $1040.00.

Now suppose it looks as if there will be 5% inflation over each of the next two years (perhaps because there was 5% inflation last year). With a conventional fixed-dollar-terms loan, we will agree on a 7% nominal interest rate. I will agree to repay $70.00 next year and $1070.00 the following year. But if inflation is actually 8% over the first year and 10% over the second year, the first payment will only be worth $70.00/1.08 = $64.81 in real terms, and the second payment will only be worth $1070.00/(1.08 X 1.10) = $900.67. In real terms the repayments total $965.48. The unanticipated inflation transfers $74.52 worth of purchasing power from you to me. You have not even received any real return on your savings.

With a variable-rate loan, only the first interest payment is determined by the 7% interest rate. The second will be determined by short-term rates at the end of the first year. Since the economy has just experienced an 8% inflation, inflationary expectations may have risen to this figure. If the real interest rate is still 2%, the nominal rate will have risen to 10%, so the final repayment will be $1100.00 instead of $1070.00. In real terms you will receive $70.00/1.08 + $1100.00/(1.08 X 1.10) = $64.81 + $925.93 = $990.74. With the variable-rate loan, $49.26 worth of purchasing power is still transferred from you to me by the unanticipated part of the inflation. The transfer is not as large as with the conventional loan, but you still have not even received any interest.

With a purchasing-power loan, I agree to pay you $20.00 times the price index next year and $1020.00 times the price index the year after. Next year the index is 1.08, so the first payment is $21.60. The second year the index is 1.08 X 1.10 = 1.188, so the second payment is $1211.76. In real terms, the total value of the repayments works out to be just $20.00 + $1020.00 = $1040.00, as it would have been if we had been confident of a constant price level. The debtor–creditor redistribution of income is entirely eliminated. If there is unanticipated inflation, your savings are not eroded. If there is unanticipated deflation, I am not saddled with a debt burden that may be beyond my means to repay.

It is a mystery why purchasing-power loans have not caught on. It is true that not everyone will prefer purchasing-power loans. For one thing, it is a nuisance to find the latest price index and be dividing by it all the time. Some people, for reasons of their own, would simply prefer to have 7% for sure rather than "risk" getting only 2% if prices level off. Perhaps they regard tangible dollars as more certain in value than some statistician's price index—a reasonable position, given the ambiguity of "the price level." Surely people who want to make dollar-denominated loans should be allowed to continue to do so.

The fact remains that a sizeable fraction of the population regard a reasonable price index as more stable in value than nominal dollars, especially in these relatively inflationary times.[†] It is puzzling that banks do not come forward with indexed savings accounts and certificates to attract their money, and lend this money back out to homebuyers and companies in indexed form. The answer probably lies in banking regulation, which is understandably resistant to untried novelties, considering the stakes and the number of people involved. Economists have been talking about indexation now for about a hundred years. Perhaps within our own lifetimes regulators will finally get used to the idea and permit this type of financial instrument.[†]

One problem with indexation is deciding on an index to use, since any two indices will report different inflation rates. The Consumer Price Index would seem like a reasonable choice, but there is a movement afoot to change its base. Currently, it records the cost of living of urban blue collar and clerical workers, but it is proposed to expand it to include the spending habits of a broader segment of the population, including the elderly, professionals, and people on welfare. If a contract is made when the CPI had one definition, and then its definition is changed, is the contract still binding? There is also talk of the Bureau of Labor Statistics'

[†] In a poll of undergraduates at Boston College, 18 out of 39 not abstaining indicated they would prefer to put their savings into purchasing power form at 2%, while 21 would prefer a fixed dollar return of 12%, assuming 10% was the best estimate of future inflation.

[‡] The House of Representatives has already taken action on variable-rate mortgages—by voting to *prohibit* Federally chartered Savings and Loan Associations from offering borrowers this partial protection against falling interest rates (May, 1975).

publishing a whole series of CPI's, representing the spending habits of several different segments of the population. In that case, which one should be used? Making the CPI a legally binding part of long-term contracts may turn its calculation into a political football instead of an objective computation. However difficult these problems are, they are not insurmountable.

A more serious problem is that of price controls. Even though these do not prevent the value of the dollar from falling, they can keep this depreciation from showing up in price indices, as was pointed out in Chapter 3. The borrower and lender in a loan contract have no say over whether Congress decides to impose price controls, so they have no way to prevent a situation in which the CPI fails to register the full change in value of the dollar. Nowadays the Democrats accept price controls in principle, while the Republicans accept them in practice, so a recurrence of controls in the future is almost inevitable. This folly on the part of both parties greatly threatens the ability of the public to defend itself against price level uncertainty when borrowing and lending.

THE INFLATIONARY REDISTRIBUTION OF INCOME: THE TAX ON REAL CASH BALANCES

The second type of income redistribution caused by inflation transfers purchasing power from the owners of real cash balances to the money-issuing agency or agencies. We have already discussed the receiving end of this transfer during the discussion of inflationary finance back in Chapter 5. Where do the resources raised by inflationary finance come from? They do not come out of the lost purchasing power of savers and pensioners, because the losses of these creditors are exactly equal to the gains of debtors whose real indebtedness has been reduced. "People on fixed incomes" are often pointed to as the losers whenever the government practices excessive monetary expansion. They do indeed lose, but their losses are the gains of the people who owe them these sums, rather than the gains of the government that is busy printing dollar bills. The fact that they are impoverished is incidental to the inflationary process. Inflationary finance would work just as well in a country in which no one happened to be in debt and no one was owed money as it would in a country with a large rentier class.

The gains from inflationary finance *can* be thought of as corresponding to losses incurred by the owners of real cash balances, a much broader segment of the population than the set of retirees, thrifty savers, and so on. To see this, suppose first that there is a positive monetary expansion rate of $\Delta M/M$, yielding real inflationary finance revenues equal to $\Delta M/P$. If velocity is constant, the quantity equation implies that this expansion causes an inflation rate of

$$\frac{\Delta P}{P} = \frac{\Delta M}{M} - \frac{\Delta y}{y} \tag{7-1}$$

As prices rise, the purchasing power of the dollars you are holding for transactions purposes falls. In real terms, the yearly depreciation of cash balances is equal to this inflation rate times M/P, the total real value of the cash balances held by everyone in the economy. Using Eq. (7-1), this depreciation is

$$\frac{\Delta P}{P} \cdot \frac{M}{P} = \left(\frac{\Delta M}{M} - \frac{\Delta y}{y}\right) \cdot \frac{M}{P} \tag{7-2}$$

$$= \frac{\Delta M}{M} - \frac{\Delta y}{y} \cdot \frac{M}{P} \tag{7-3}$$

On the other hand, with no monetary expansion, there will be zero inflationary finance revenues. If velocity is constant, inflation will be

$$\frac{\Delta P}{P} = - \frac{\Delta y}{y} \tag{7-4}$$

The yearly depreciation of cash balances will then be

$$\frac{\Delta P}{P} \cdot \frac{M}{P} = - \frac{\Delta y}{y} \cdot \frac{M}{P} \tag{7-5}$$

(Since inflation is negative, this depreciation will be negative as well.)

The difference between expression (7-3) and the right-hand side of Eq. (7-5) is just $\Delta M/P$, the government's revenue from monetary expansion. When inflationary finance increases the government's purchasing power by $\Delta M/P$, the purchasing power of owners of dollar bills decreases by precisely the same amount. In this manner, inflationary finance is said to act as a *tax on real cash balances*. The resources the government (and the counterfeiter) gets by printing money do not appear out of thin air. Rather, they are taken away from the public, just as if the income tax had been raised or your pocket had been picked.

To be perfectly honest, the magic of this coincidence required a little sleight of hand on our part. The above calculation is valid only if real cash balances M/P are equal with and without the inflation. The loss to money owners from the inflation is just equal to the gain to the government, minus the amount money owners would have gained from the zero expansion deflation, assuming (unreasonably) that they would hold no greater cash balances during the deflation than during the inflation. In truth, money owners lose *more* than the government gains. First, they have to put up with the inconvenience of reduced real cash balances, since inflationary expectations induce higher velocity. Then, on top of that, they lose the sum the government gains.[†]

THE WELFARE COST OF INFLATION

An ordinary excise tax transfers resources from the public to the government, and in the process induces in inefficient allocation of resources. Because of this inefficiency, the public actually loses more in welfare terms than the government gains. This "dead-weight" welfare loss is not picked up as a gain to anyone else. It is simply a loss to society as a whole. A similar welfare loss is caused by inflation. As the inflation rate rises, people devote a greater and greater portion of their own time and other resources to keeping their real cash balances down. Workers begin to be paid once a week instead of once a month, then once a day, and even

[†] Today the Federal Government happens to be the largest single debtor in the country. It therefore stands to gain from inflation by having the real burden of this indebtedness reduced as well as through inflationary finance. These two effects should not be confused.

several times each day. As soon as money is received, it is rushed to the stores to buy something—anything—before its value disappears. Martin Bailey has estimated that the resources thus wasted may run as high as 50% of the resources actually diverted to the government with revenue-maximizing fully anticipated inflation. This ratio becomes considerably smaller for lower steady-state inflation rates, and even higher for runaway inflations.

Some economists belittle the welfare cost of inflation:

> According to economic theory, the ultimate social cost of antici-pated inflation is the wasteful use of resources to economize hold-ings of currency and other noninterest-bearing means of payment. I suspect that intelligent laymen would be utterly astounded if they realized that *this* is the great evil economists are talking about. They have imagined a much more devastating cataclysm, with Vesuvius vengefully punishing the sinners below. Extra trips between savings banks and commercial banks. What an anti-climax![†]

We can't guarantee anything as dramatic as Vesuvius. However, runaway inflation could easily become so acute that indirect exchange would vir-tually disappear from the economy. In that case, we would revert to barter and the problems that entails as discussed in Chapter 1. The welfare cost of the inflation could then be measured by the quiet despair of the primor-dial skate key quandary, illustrated on the back cover.

As a rule, the distortions caused by taxing up a given quantity of real resources are smaller if a small tax is levied on a large tax base than if a large tax is levied on one or two items. The services provided by real cash balances are ordinarily only a small item in the economy, though like many other small items in the economy, they would be sorely missed if done without altogether. Therefore, concentrating government revenue creation on cash balances by relying on the printing press to the exclusion of other taxes is highly inefficient. It would be most sensible to rely on monetary expansion (which is not necessarily inflationary if no greater

[†] James Tobin, "Inflation and Unemployment," *American Economic Review* (March, 1972), p. 15.

than the real growth of the economy) to finance at most a few percent of the government's activities.

THE INFLATIONARY REDISTRIBUTION OF INCOME: THE INFLATIONARY PROCESS

A third and less well-known redistribution of income arises in the course of the inflationary process itself.

Suppose the counterfeiter in Chapter 2 uses his newly printed money to buy a new wardrobe. As far as his haberdasher is concerned, the monetary expansion and ensuing inflation are beneficial. The haberdasher can move his suits more quickly and get top prices for them. When he takes his profits down to buy a new car, he finds that his demand pushes car prices up a little bit. But he is still better off, because he is near (in an economic sense) to the source of the new money. The goods he sells go up in price more than the goods he buys. Furthermore, the goods he sells go up sooner than the goods he buys. Likewise, the automobile manufacturers and auto workers will probably benefit, along with other interest groups who are near to the point of injection of the inflationary money.

As we follow the effects of the new money through the economy, we eventually start to encounter people who are just breaking even. Construction workers, for example, may find an increased demand for their services on the part of haberdashers and auto workers. They are still able to buy food relatively cheaply, but already have been paying higher prices for clothing and cars. Their incomes rise, but their cost of living has already risen substantially, since they are competing for goods with the ever-widening circle of people whose incomes have gone up. They lose as much command over resources before their incomes rise as they gain after they rise. Finally, we come to people whose incomes don't rise until after their cost of living has gone up, and then only by the same amount. These people clearly lose. For example, if the counterfeiter and haberdasher increase their consumption of food only slightly, food prices are likely to be among the last to rise. But meanwhile, farmers find clothing, automobiles, and buildings more expensive. Their real income will have fallen as a result of the inflation.

The debate will rage, with one side arguing that inflation is beneficial, because it is "good for business," while the other side contends that it is harmful, because "incomes don't keep up with the cost of living." Happily, we may conclude that both sides are right. Inflation is good for some people's business, precisely to the extent that other people's incomes don't keep up with the cost of living. Whether new paper money is introduced into the economy legally or illegally, it does not create any new resources. What it does do is transfer purchasing power from those at the end of the line to those at the front.

If the monetary expansion is permanent, so that people come to expect the inflation perfectly, part of this redistribution will go away as homebuilders and farmers start to mark up their prices automatically without waiting for persistent excess demand. However, there will still be some permanent transfer in favor of those who produce the particular goods purchased by the recipients of the inflationary finance revenue, and away from the rest of the economy.

INFLATION AND ECONOMIC CALCULATION

Inflation does funny things to economic calculation. It is said that during the German hyperinflation of 1922-1923, prices were rising so fast that you could get more for an empty beer bottle than you paid for it full a few days earlier.[†] Suppose you sell your home (at a fantastic profit in nominal terms) and invest in this very lucrative business. You pore ("pour?") over your work from dawn to dusk and then from dusk to dawn. You make thousands, even millions of marks. But for all your dedication, you would end up on skid row in a short time, a dissipated victim of "money illusion."

In a typical investment, costs precede receipts. If the price level is constant, one merely needs to ask whether receipts exceed costs in order to decide whether the investment is "profitable." But when there is inflation, the later receipts will have less value per dollar than the earlier

[†]Richard Hughes, *The Fox in the Attic* (New York: Signet, 1963), pp. 96–97.

costs. In order to determine whether an investment is advantageous, costs and receipts must be divided by subsequent values of an appropriate price index in order to reduce them to base year dollars with equal purchasing power. If this is not done (and it usually is not), economic calculation is falsified. Too great a portion of the receipts will be interpreted as profit income, instead of a return of capital. This falsification of economic calculation has two immediate effects: first, it means that people will tend to squander scarce productive resources on investments that, in constant dollars, would be seen to be unsound; second, people will overestimate their income, and tend to overconsume and undersave.

Private citizens have an incentive to see through this money illusion and to base their actions on calculations that adjust for the depreciation of money. For instance, in postwar Germany, many firms kept their accounts in terms of foreign currencies that were more stable in value than the mark, and therefore were not tempted to pay excessive dividends to their stockholders.

However, the Internal Revenue Service has no incentive to be so cagey. Accounts kept in current dollars show higher profits and yield more taxes. Hence, a dollar is a dollar, so far as the tax collector is concerned. Because the income tax is based on current dollar accounting, inflation turns the income tax into a tax on capital. Part of what should be figured as capital turns up as income in the accounts, and is taxed just as if it were true profit income. Consequently, if the tax rate and the inflation rate are sufficiently high compared to the real rate of return on capital, the real rate of return *after tax* may actually be negative. Once this happens, there will be no further incentive to invest. Hoarding consumer goods will at least give a zero real rate of return, so why buy corporate stock? Savings will dry up and the real capital stock of the nation will dwindle as existing capital equipment depreciates.

Savings are the source of the growth of the capital stock available to the economy. This growth in the capital stock in turn helps make possible the secular growth of real wages that we have come to take for granted. With constant or declining capital and a growing population, real wages would instead fall, to the point where starvation held population growth in check. We would live in the world of famine described by Malthus. Fortunately, Malthus was wrong. Ordinarily, people will save enough to make labor income grow faster than population. However, the possibility of capital stagnation, induced by inflation in conjunction with a dollar-accounting income tax, is a very serious prospect.

If we know the real rate of return on capital and the effective marginal tax rate, we can easily calculate the inflation rate that will just cut off investment. Let t be the tax rate (as a fraction of unity), and let r be the real rate of return to equity investment. We wish to find the inflation rate x that just means investors break even in real terms, after taxes. The measured nominal rate of return on this investment will be the real return, plus the inflation rate:

$$r + x \tag{7-6}$$

The tax collector will take t times $(r + x)$, which leaves the investor with

$$(1 - t) \cdot (r + x) \tag{7-7}$$

as his *nominal* yield after taxes. The real yield is the nominal yield minus inflation, so he is left with

$$(1 - t)(r + x) - x \tag{7-8}$$

in real terms after taxes. To find the critical inflation rate, we set expression (7-8) equal to zero and solve for x:

$$(1 - t)(r + x) - x = 0$$
$$r - rt + x - xt - x = 0$$
$$r(1 - t) = xt$$
$$x = \frac{(1 - t)}{t} r \tag{7-9}$$

Let us illustrate formula (7-9) with some numerical examples. Suppose the real rate of return on equity investment (e.g., corporate stock) is

8%. The marginal tax rate for a sole proprietor of moderate means might be about 33%, or 1/3. With these figures, the critical inflation rate is

$$x = \frac{(1 - 1/3)}{1/3} (8\%)$$

$$= \frac{2/3}{1/3}(8\%)$$

$$= 2(8\%)$$

$$= 16\% \text{ per annum}$$

This rate is only a little higher than the inflation we realized during 1974.

Now consider corporate investment, instead of investment by a sole proprietor. The corporation must pay taxes of approximately 50% before it can pay out dividends, and then the stockholder must pay personal income tax on the dividends. If the stockholder is again in the 33% bracket, he may keep only 2/3 of 1/2, or 1/3, of the original nominal profits. In effect, he is paying taxes of 2/3, or 67%. Using this marginal tax rate, and the same value for r, we find

$$x = \frac{(1 - 2/3)}{2/3}(8\%)$$

$$= \frac{1/3}{2/3}(8\%)$$

$$= \frac{1}{2}(8\%)$$

$$= 4\%$$

Ah, for the good old days of only 4% inflation!

These figures suggest that we are now on the verge of a situation where serious long-term repercussions will set in if taxation is not reformed to prevent taxation of capital. It is probably too early to say whether the decline in real income that began in 1974 is the result of this effect.[†]

[†] The published "real income" figures are actually too high in inflationary times, since they include the real value of profits calculated using undeflated dollars.

Problem 7-1

If the effective marginal tax rate is 25%, while the real rate of return on equity investment is 6%, what is the inflation rate at which capital stagnation sets in?

THE POLEMICS OF INFLATION

Inflation and attempts to stop inflation have the additional side effect of generating a lot of verbiage. The "old-fashioned" view was that inflation is caused by excessive monetary expansion, which in turn reflects something seedy in the state of public morality. This attitude was expressed by Madame de Staël on her return to Austria in 1812, after it had come under the control of her archenemy Napoleon:

> I no longer found the same honesty in the people that had struck me four years earlier; paper money stimulates the imagination with hopes of rapid and easy gain, and the hazards of chance upset the steady, even flow of existence, the basis for honesty in the common people. During my stay in Austria a man was hanged for forging counterfeit money just after the old notes had been replaced; on his way to the gallows he cried out that it was not he who had stolen, but the state.†

The "modern" view, which is not particularly new, but which has gained respectability since the publication of Keynes's *General Theory* in 1936, contends that the link between money and inflation is extremely weak if it exists at all, and that even if there were such a link, inflation is a far lesser evil than the unemployment that might be caused by monetary restriction. Nobel Prize winning economist Paul Samuelson reflected this position in his column in *Newsweek*:

> For there is no sight in the world more awful than that of an oldtime economist, foam-flecked at the mouth and hell-bent to cure inflation

†Madame de Staël, *Ten Years of Exile* (New York: Saturday Review Press, 1972), p. 143.

by monetary discipline. God willing, we shan't soon see his like again.[†]

The "modern" view was put forward even more forcefully by William Jennings Bryan in his 1896 campaign to replace the gold standard with a bimetallic gold-silver standard. Foam-flecked at the mouth and hell-bent to cure unemployment and alleviate indebtedness by monetary expansion, he preached his gospel at every whistle-stop in the land:

> You shall not press down upon the brow of labor this crown of thorns, you shall not crucify mankind upon a cross of gold.[†]

The pessimist may conclude that there are no options open to society intermediate between crucifixion on a cross of gold and immolation on a pyre of paper. It is hoped that this short book has cast a little light, albeit monochromatic, on this debate.

REFERENCES

For background on indexation, see Thomas M. Humphrey, "The Concept of Indexation in the History of Economic Thought," *Economic Review* of the Federal Reserve Bank of Richmond (Nov./Dec., 1974). Many of the consequences of inflation are discussed by Reuben Kessel and Armen Alchian in their article "Effects of Inflation," *Journal of Political Economy* (December, 1962). The classic article on the welfare cost of inflationary finance is the one by Martin Bailey, cited at the end of Chapter 5. The falsification of economic calculation as a consequence of inflation is a favorite theme of Ludwig von Mises. See, for instance, *The Theory of Money and Credit*, pp. 195–212, 223. Pages 219–224 and 426–428 of that book comprise a spirited polemic against inflationary finance.

Terms to Remember

The three inflationary redistributions of income
Purchasing power loans

[†]June, 1969; quoted in *The Samuelson Sampler* (Thomas Horton and Daughters, 1973), p. 55.
[‡]William Jennings Bryan, *The First Battle* (Chicago, Illinois: Conkey, 1896), p. 206.

Variable-interest-rate loans
Indexation
The tax on real cash balances
The welfare cost of inflation
Money illusion
Capital stagnation

SOLUTIONS

Stop! Make every effort to work the problems through to a numerical solution before you look at the solutions.

$$P = \frac{Q_a^1 P_a^2 + Q_b^1 P_b^2}{Q_a^1 P_a^1 + Q_b^1 P_b^1} = \frac{(2)(12) + (4)(9)}{(2)(11) + (4)(7)}$$

$$= \frac{24 + 36}{22 + 28} = \frac{60}{50}$$

$$= 1.20$$

(If you got 1.14, you made the mistake of using different quantities in the numerator and denominator, and therefore got the growth of nominal income instead of the price level. If you got $57/46 = 1.24$, you used period 2 quantities, which are just as good in theory as period 1 quantities.

That they should give a different answer shows that there is an element of ambiguity in any price index. Whichever way it is computed, note that some of the quantity data are not used.)

Problem 2-2

$$\frac{\Delta P}{P} = \frac{3.00 - 2.50}{2.50}$$

$$= \frac{0.50}{2.50}$$

$$= \frac{1}{5}$$

$$= 0.20 \text{ or } 20\%$$

Problem 3-1

We have

$$\frac{\Delta M}{M} + \frac{\Delta V}{V} = \frac{\Delta P}{P} + \frac{\Delta y}{y}$$

so

$$\frac{\Delta V}{V} = \frac{\Delta P}{P} + \frac{\Delta y}{y} - \frac{\Delta M}{M}$$

$$= (0.01) + (0.04) - (0.06)$$

$$= -0.01$$

Velocity must have fallen by 1%.

Problem 3-2

$$\frac{\Delta M}{M} = \frac{\Delta P}{P} + \frac{\Delta y}{y} - \frac{\Delta V}{V}$$

$$= (0) + (0.05) - (-0.03)$$

$$= 0.08 \text{ or } 8\%$$

(Note: If you got 2% instead, you probably forgot to cancel out the two minus signs.)

Problem 3-3

$$\frac{\Delta y}{y} = \frac{\Delta M}{M} + \frac{\Delta V}{V} - \frac{\Delta P}{P}$$

$$= (0.08) + (0.01) - (0.06)$$

$$= 0.03 \text{ or } 3\%$$

Problem 4-1

$$\frac{(\Delta P)}{(P)^*} = i - r$$

$$= (0.04) - (0.06)$$

$$= -0.02$$

so people expect 2% *deflation.*

Problem 4-2

r is not much affected by inflationary expectations so it would remain roughly 6%. Then

$$i = (0.06) + (0.03)$$

$$= 0.09 \text{ or } 9\%$$

Problem 5-1

For each interest rate, calculate the expected inflation rate. By assumption, this equals the actual inflation rate, so you may then calculate the corresponding monetary expansion rate. Multiply that by the real cash balance demand and you have the real resources raised:

$i\,(\%)$	$\left(\dfrac{\Delta P}{P}\right)^{*} = \dfrac{\Delta P}{P}\,(\%)$	$\dfrac{\Delta M}{M}\,(\%)$	m (millions of 1967 pesos)	g (millions of 1967 pesos)
5	-5	0	200	0
10	0	5	180	9
15	+5	10	160	16
20	10	15	140	21
25	15	20	120	24
30	20	25	100	25
35	25	30	80	24
40	30	35	60	21
45	35	40	40	16
50	40	45	20	9

A monetary expansion rate of 25% will result in 20% inflation, and will yield 25 million 1967 pesos worth of resources per year.

Problem 5-2

$$\text{(a)} \quad i = 10\% + 0 = 10\%$$

$$m = \$180 \text{ million } (1967)$$

$$\frac{\Delta M}{M} = \frac{36}{180} = 0.20 \text{ (or } 20\%)$$

$$\frac{\Delta P}{P} = 20\% + 0 - 5\% = 15\%$$

(b) $i = 10\% + 15\% = 25\%$

$m = \$120$ million (1967)

$\dfrac{\Delta M}{M} = \dfrac{36}{120} = 0.30$ (or 30%)

$\dfrac{\Delta P}{P} = 30\% + 0 - 5\% = 25\%$

(c) $i = 10\% + 25\% = 35\%$

$m = \$80$ million (1967)

$\dfrac{\Delta M}{M} = \dfrac{36}{80} = 0.45$ (or 45%)

$\dfrac{\Delta P}{P} = 45\% + 0 - 5\% = 40\%$

(d) $i = 10\% + 40\% = 50\%$

$m = \$20$ million (1967)

$\dfrac{\Delta M}{M} = \dfrac{36}{20} = 1.8$ (or 180%)

$\dfrac{\Delta P}{P} = 180\% + 0 - 5\% = 175\%!$

(Note: With these figures, the maximum revenue obtainable with fully anticipated inflation was 25 million 1967 pesos. When the target is set higher than this figure, at 36 million, there *must* be runaway inflation.)

Problem 6-1

(a) U_n occurs when $\Delta P/P = (\Delta P/P)^*$, so

$$0 = 8 - 2U_n$$

$$2U_n = 8$$

$$U_n = 4$$

The natural rate is 4%.

(b) $\dfrac{\Delta P}{P} = 8 - 2U + (\dfrac{\Delta P}{P})^*$

$= 8 - 2(2) + (0)$

$= 4$

or 4% inflation.

(c) $\dfrac{\Delta P}{P} = 8 - 2(2) + (4)$

$= 8$

or 8% inflation.

Problem 7-1

The critical inflation rate will be

$$x = \frac{(1 - 1/4)}{1/4}(6\%)$$

$$= 3\,(6\%)$$

$$= 18\%$$

INDEX

117